Praise for
Keith's Clinical Reasoning Resources

From Nurse Educators:

"I just finished my first clinical rotation of using Keith's Clinical Reasoning Template instead of our traditional care plan. Great success! The students loved it, I loved it, and they report feeling much better prepared for patient care. I've been using Keith's case studies for the past couple of years. I've decreased my PowerPoint time to allow case studies during class. The students love it, and our class time is much more productive. They score higher on their exams because of the application."

–Rob Morris, RN, MSN
Nursing Faculty
College of the Sequoias, Visalia, California

"Having worked with Keith and having watched the development of these clinical reasoning case studies, I can say that they work. The students were engaged, and the second-year students who had Keith last year continue to talk about them."

–Michelle Natrop, RN, MSN
Nursing Faculty
Normandale Community College, Bloomington, Minnesota

"Your clinical reasoning case studies help students to apply information and look at the big picture. I had so much fun teaching using this approach and I didn't see anyone nodding off in the back of the class!"

–Janet Miller, MA, RN
Nursing Faculty
Hibbing Community College, Hibbing, Minnesota

"I have adapted and utilized your thinking tools for clinical and I have seen a tremendous increase in the clinical decision-making abilities of my students."

–Leeann Denning, DNP, RN, CNE
Assistant Professor
Shawnee State University, Portsmouth, Ohio

"I have been using your clinical reasoning case studies with my second-year nursing students. The students have said that they really like the case studies as it makes them really have to think through the important physiologic concepts as well as apply what they know."

–Linden Fraser, RN, MSN
Nursing Faculty
Nicolet College, Rhinelander, Wisconsin

"I implemented Keith's clinical reasoning case study on pneumonia/COPD. The students LOVED it. They were so engrossed in it that when I told them it was time to stop and discuss, for the first time ever, they asked for extra time to complete it!"

–Cynthia Sterling-Fox, RN, MSN, FNP-C
Assistant Professor of Nursing
CUNY Medgar Evers College, Brooklyn, New York

"I used your handout 'Clinical Reasoning Questions to Develop Nurse Thinking' today with my practical nursing students and they loved it! It made them feel like they were better prepared to care for their patients."

–Priscilla Anderson, RN
Assistant Professor of Nursing
NHTI Concord's Community College, New Hampshire

Clinical Dilemmas

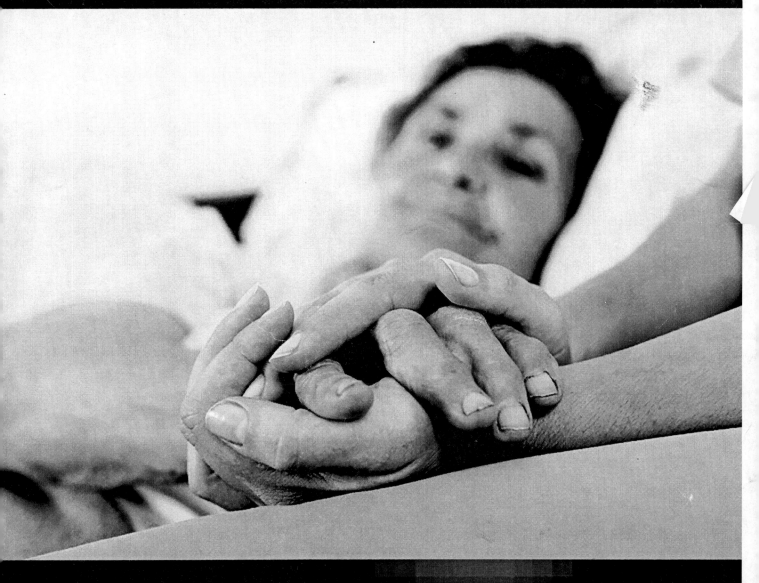

Case Studies that Cultivate Caring, Civility & Clinical Reasoning

Keith Rischer, RN, MA, CEN, CCRN

Clinical Dilemmas

Case Studies that Cultivate Caring, Civility & Clinical Reasoning

Author: Keith Rischer, RN, MA, CEN, CCRN

Table of Contents

Authors Preface

Where's the Caring?

This rhetorical question was recently the title of an editorial in *Nurse Educator* (Serber, 2014), by an educator who has noted a recent erosion of caring behaviors in nurses. Serber believes that one of the reasons for this can be traced back to how nurses are taught. From her perspective, nursing education tends to emphasize the science of nursing and minimizes the importance of the "art" of nursing that includes caring. It does not integrate caring and the "art" of nursing in the curriculum. I have observed in the programs where I have taught that caring is expected of the student, but is not integrated and taught. Instead it is assumed to be "caught" and left to chance. In the past, this approach may have been acceptable because the primary motivation for most students to enter nursing was NOT for the money or job security, but that they had a strong comportment of caring and a desire to serve others. As nursing becomes a higher-paid profession with increasing security and demand, caring may not be the primary motivator for students who choose to enter nursing education as it once was. Therefore, it is imperative to longer assume that the "art" can be caught, but must be practically integrated in the curriculum and taught.

I have written this unique series of case studies, "Clinical Dilemmas," that emphasize and integrate the "art" of nursing that includes caring, spiritual care, nurse engagement/presence, and ethical decision making and its relevance to nursing practice. Each case study also emphasizes the essence of clinical reasoning that includes the need to identify the essence of the current situation and relevant clinical data, and determine the nursing priority with resultant interventions.

These case studies can be used in the classroom as an active learning tool to develop the ethical comportment of nurses as well as post-conference in the clinical setting. These case studies are derived from themes I have experienced in clinical practice and represent the most common clinical dilemmas a nurse will likely encounter in practice. They are divided into the following four categories:

PATIENT dilemmas

- How should the nurse best respond to a terminal patient in spiritual distress? a depressed patient who has given up hope? or a patient with narcotic addiction who may be be demonstrating drug-seeking behavior?

TREATMENT dilemmas

- How to best support a patient/family who is faced with permanent, life altering therapies such as dialysis or conservative medical management that may increase the risk of dying.

ETHICAL dilemmas

- How to recognize concerns of medical futility and how to respond appropriately and how to respect the autonomy of the patient in the absence of a living will.

NURSING dilemmas

- How to effectively address incivility by another nurse, student or faculty member and how to develop self-care to prevent burnout.

There are typically ten questions for each case study. This is one simple strategy that can be effective to encourage responsibility for student learning and engage them at the same time:

- Divide the class into ten small groups of three to four students (depending on size). Make this random so other students who do not normally mix together do so.
- Assign one to two questions from the clinical reasoning case study to each group.
- Give time for students to collaborate using textbooks or other resources to answer their assigned questions.
- Have each group present their answers to class and discuss rationale for the answers they chose.

This same principle can be used in post conference in the clinical setting by having each student take responsibility to answer one question and then dialogue as a clinical group.

These salient scenarios will engage students and provide needed dialogue in nursing. Just as clinical skills such as sterile technique must be practiced by students in order to become proficient, thinking and the difficult dilemmas students will experience also need to be rehearsed and practiced to develop needed proficiency to navigate these sometimes difficult situations. By intentionalizing the "art" of nursing, educators can be proactive and teach the current generation of nursing students not only the science of nursing, but the historical legacy and centrality of caring and the "art" of nursing and its relevance to practice today.

Though each clinical dilemma case study includes a fully developed answer key that is supported by the literature as well as my observations in clinical practice, use it only as a guide and do not hesitate to integrate what you have learned and observed in your clinical experience to teach them as your own. Though there are principles to guide the practice of the "art" of nursing, every nurse is unique and will integrate and incorporate differently. Use each open ended question of the case study to facilitate student dialogue and discussion.

If you have found these case studies helpful, have suggestions as to how they could be improved, or have a question, please do not hesitate to contact me. I hope to hear from you soon!

Keith, RN

Email: Keith@KeithRN.com

References

Serber, S. (2014). Nurses: Where's the caring? *Nurse Educator, 39*(1), 15-16.

Foreword

How do you teach the "soft skills" related to nursing practice? We all know about them, but may struggle with integration of realistic clinical experiences in the classroom. Keith has presented a new series of clinical activities that offer an "easy" way to begin these conversations online, in the classroom or in the clinical setting with students. Each scenario has a well-thought-out instructor's key along with a student version with insightful questions that will cultivate needed thinking and discussion. The relevance of these activities to nursing education include the following points of consideration:

1. Nurses face ethical dilemmas regularly in practice. The overlays of how to teach, sorting out the "main thing" or essence of the current dilemma, caring responses, and how to be sensitive and effective as a nurse are threaded throughout.

2. Educators are aware of the need to develop cultural sensitivity to special populations (i.e. aging, ethnic, military, etc.) and these clinical activities will help the learners develop an awareness of their unique needs during a health crisis.

3. There are many overlays of psychiatric principles such as therapeutic communication that are relevant in all practice settings. Anxiety, depression, and drug seeking behavior are the "soft stuff" that nurses will see regularly in practice and need to be prepared to effectively manage and support. Keith goes there in a relevant way to teach with well-written, deep-thinking scenarios for the student.

Nurse educators seeking to teach with clinical relevance in the classroom will welcome this workbook with scenarios taken from clinical practice that knit current evidence and theory into the instructor's key. The connections between clinical practice and theory are laced together and readily apparent.

Finally, there are cases on incivility in nursing as well as academia. After reading the cases Keith wrote on incivility, I realized I deal with it on a daily basis, regularly work through it, and am not the only one who experiences situations when the student is unaware of their unacceptable, uncivil behaviors.

Thank you, Keith, for bringing this powerful collection of clinical reasoning case studies that contextualize clinical dilemmas that are salient, realistic and encourage discovery learning in the classroom. This is a needed resource to begin this journey easily with a map and a compass to help us teach the art of nursing.

–Barbara Hill, RN, MSN, CNE, CMSRN
Associate Professor
Community College of Baltimore County, Baltimore, Maryland

Introduction

"The spirit in which she does her work makes all the difference. Invested as she should with the dignity of her profession and the cloak of love for suffering humanity, she can ennoble anything her hand may be called upon to do, and for work done in this spirit there will ever come to her a recompense far outweighing that of silver and gold."

–Isabel Hampton Robb, 1900

Founder of the American Nurses Association, American Journal of Nursing, & National League for Nursing

"Caring practices are central to nursing. What it is to nurse cannot be separated from what it is to care for and about others."

–Christine A. Tanner, PhD, RN, FAAN, former editor Journal of Nursing Education

---

Before you use this resource in your program, please take the time to read my introduction that highlights the importance of the "art" of nursing and its ongoing relevance to the profession today. The themes that are integrated in each case study are presented here in additional depth to deepen learning of this most important content in nursing education. In this introduction I highlight the following foundational components of the "art" of nursing that include:

- Caring
- Nurse engagement
- Spiritual care
- Nurse presence

Caring has traditionally been viewed as the essence of nursing practice and the most important characteristic of a nurse (Leininger, 1988). Caring is also a distinct, dominant, central, and unifying focus for nursing practice (Leininger, 1991). Caring as a recognized core value in nursing is not new. It was emphasized at the beginning of the modern era by influential nurse educator Isabel Hampton Robb, who later went on to found the American Nurses Association, the *American Journal of Nursing*, and what would later become the National League for Nursing.

While Hampton Robb stated in the language of her day that nurses should provide care by embracing *"the dignity of her profession and the cloak of love for suffering humanity,"* (see quote above) it is important to recognize that this must NOT be treated as an abstract philosophical platitude. We need to encourage our students to not only embrace this ethic, but also see it as a philosophical truth that must also be lived out (Benner, 2013) by seeing each patient as a valued person with whom they share a common humanity.

Though the emphasis in nursing education today is knowledge acquisition and skill development, this in itself is not enough. Every student must CARE and have COMPASSION for others. Patricia Benner also affirms that caring is central to nursing practice. *"Nursing can never be reduced to mere technique…the nature of the caring relationship is central to most nursing interventions"* (Benner & Wrubel, 1989, p. 4). *"The nurse is both a knowledge worker and one who cares…knowledge is dangerous if it is divorced from caring"* (p. 400). Caring is an essential component of expert practice that has the power to not only impact the patient but enrich the nurse in the process (Benner & Wrubel, 1988). This is the unique legacy of the nursing profession throughout history, including the modern era ushered in by Nightingale.

Benefits of Caring

Nursing literature and research have conclusively shown that the patients of a caring, engaged nurse have better outcomes (Swanson, 1999). Caring gives the nurse a heightened sense of awareness and guides the evaluation of nursing interventions by recognizing subtle changes in the patient's condition. In this context of caring, the nurse pays close attention to the patient's body language, facial expressions, and tone of voice and interprets the significance of what is communicated (Benner & Wrubel, 1989). When the head and heart are integrated and fully engaged in practice, the nurse clearly communicates in both verbal and nonverbal ways that each person matters and recognizes EARLY changes that may signify a change in status.

Some patients lose hope and a sense of connection to others as a result of their illness and do not feel that they matter. When the nurse demonstrates that the patient matters, this has the power to reintegrate the patient with his or her world. Being approachable and available is central to effective nursing care and an essential ingredient to patient recovery (Orlick & Benner, 1988).

Caring behaviors also create healing environments that positively influence and improve patient outcomes. The benefits patients receive when they experience caring by the nurse include enhanced healing, decreased length of stay, increased well-being and physical comfort. Caring influences nurse engagement, which makes the nurse observe the effectiveness of interventions and notice subtle signs of patient improvement or deterioration (Benner & Wrubel, 1988). Practicing in a caring manner also benefits the nurse and enhances the nurse's well-being, both personally and professionally. The nurse feels more connected to his or her patients and colleagues and is more satisfied with bedside care (Swanson, 1999).

Patients can readily detect a nurse's nonverbal communication that contradicts caring behaviors. Students must learn to recognize the influence and significance of their eye contact, body language, and tone of voice with every patient encounter and how they communicate caring and contribute to a patient's well-being (Benner & Wrubel, 1989).

The Power of Two Questions

Novice nursing students are task-oriented and focused on what needs to be done for their patient (Benner, 1984). When I taught fundamental clinical, some students seemed to forget at times that there is a person in the bed! To integrate caring behaviors and make them intentional in your clinical setting, I have created two open-ended questions that require students to reflect upon and place empathy, caring, compassion, and nurse engagement in the context of the patient they are caring for.

1. *What is the patient likely experiencing/feeling right now in this situation?*

   This question emphasizes empathy, which is the ability to imagine and put oneself in another's place with the intention to understand what another feels or experiences. Empathy is a synonym of compassion and represents another perspective to situate the necessity of compassion to nursing practice.

2. *What can I do to engage myself with this patient's experience and show that they matter to me as a person?*

   This question begins with an emphasis of nurse engagement and what can be practically done to demonstrate this. The last half of this question is derived from Patricia Benner, who defines the essence of caring as a nurse as recognizing the value and worth of those you care for and that the patient and their experience matter to you. (Benner & Wrubel, 1989).

Nurse Engagement

Skillful nurse engagement complements caring and compassion and is also foundational to nursing practice and care. The nurse must remain clinically curious and responsive to the patient's story and situation. When distracted and not engaged, the nurse will be unable to invest the energy needed to recognize relevant and urgent clinical signs that may require intervention. When nurses are not engaged with the patient and their clinical problem, patient outcomes will suffer (Benner, Hooper-Kyriakidis, & Stannard, 2011).

Students must also be taught to leave personal distractions at the door once they enter the clinical environment. This is especially important for first-year students who are new to the clinical setting. If a patient can sense that the student nurse is stressed or anxious, he or she will NOT feel cared for (Swanson, 1991). Personal, family, and any other stressors or problems will affect the quality of care and nurse engagement needed for practice. Though these stressors may be difficult to fight through at times, students must learn to focus on the patient to whom they are assigned. Students must understand the need to hide their anxieties and become a good actor when the situation warrants!

Spiritual Care

By providing compassionate care, the nurse directly affects the patient's physical and emotional needs. Holistic care also involves caring for the spirit. For some students, spiritual care may conjure up images and expectations of praying with patients and going way out of their comfort zone. Though spiritual care may include prayer, it is much more. The essence of spiritual care is caring and serving the whole person: the physical, emotional, social, and spiritual aspects of their being (Murphy & Walker, 2013).

Though spiritual care is clearly within the nurse's scope of practice, I find that most students, as well as nurses in practice, are uncomfortable with this responsibility. Contributing factors to this discomfort for some may include the dominant physical/medical model in healthcare, secular-humanistic worldview of educational and healthcare institutions as well as a lack of emphasis on spiritual care in nursing education. In one survey, 87 percent of nursing programs do not have specific content on how to practically incorporate spiritual care in practice (Murphy & Walker, 2013)!

I have observed that those most comfortable with spiritual care find their own faith and spiritual traditions personally meaningful and relevant. When it comes to spirituality, you cannot give to others if you do not have something within to give. But regardless of where they are in their faith journeys, I encourage my students to embrace this responsibility in practical and nonthreatening ways so that they can holistically support and care for their patients. Just because a student may not be a participant of any faith tradition or may be an atheist or agnostic, he or she must recognize that if spirituality or a faith tradition is important to the patient, it must also be central and important to the nurse!

A practical, holistic approach to providing spiritual care in nursing recaptures the perspective that all that is done for the patient by the nurse can be an act of spiritual care. Instead of compartmentalizing patient care as "nursing interventions" and spiritual care as something you will do when you have the time, everything that is done for the patient can become a demonstration of spiritual care. For example, taking a set of vital signs becomes an opportunity for presence and spiritual assessment. The student can further intentionalize spiritual care by thinking with every interaction, *"What are this patient's needs, fears, anxieties, or questions?"* Every interaction is filled with meaning as the student engages the "entire" patient (Murphy & Walker, 2013).

Spiritual Care Made Practical

If there is an obvious need to care for the spirit by providing hope in a time of crisis, spiritual care can accomplished in just a couple minutes. Let me share a real-life example from my practice in the ED to show how this works (some details changed to protect patient confidentiality).

One of my patients, a middle-aged Hispanic woman, presented with a chief complaint of vaginal bleeding at twelve weeks gestation. She had an ultrasound that was unable to locate a fetal heartbeat or intra-uterine pregnancy. She unfortunately had a miscarriage. For this woman, this was an especially devastating event because it was not her first miscarriage, but her fourteenth without bringing a pregnancy successfully to term. She was so hopeful that this would have been the one that would result in a child she would someday hold in her arms. The primary care provider saw the patient, informed her of the ultrasound results, and promptly left the room and wrote orders to discharge the patient to home.

I came into the room a few minutes later with the discharge paperwork. She was still sobbing and in obvious distress. I had two choices. I could quickly give her the paperwork and send her home so we could see the next patient in a very busy ED, or I could acknowledge her pain, show that she mattered to someone, and offer her hope in some small tangible way. I chose the latter.

I pulled up a chair, sat down beside her in silence for several seconds. I then said, *"I am so sorry."* But I didn't just say it; I truly meant it because her experience and the loss of her fourteenth baby really did matter to me. I remembered that she made a reference earlier that her church was praying for her. There was no time to call a chaplain. I was all she had. There are going to be times in practice when all you can do is pray, and this seemed to be one of those times. I asked if I could pray for her before she left. She quickly agreed, and I did so.

Afterward she opened her eyes, wiped away a tear, looked a bit more relaxed and said, *"Thank you so much! You have no idea how much this meant to me!"* I then went through her discharge instructions and she left the ED. This nursing intervention took only a couple of minutes. Every nurse has the ability to make a lasting difference by caring not only for the physical needs, but those of the spirit as well.

Another example took place in the ICU. I recently cared for a patient who was critically ill, but beginning to make slow but steady progress. There were numerous pictures of Jesus on the wall of her room, and I asked the mother if faith was important to her daughter. She stated, *"No, I brought these pictures for me. My daughter no longer goes to church, but I am praying daily and I know that God will work all things together for good."* I acknowledged her feelings and stated that I, too, would pray for her daughter. Her face lit up with a big smile, which said more than any words.

Teach your students to pay close attention to what is in a patient's room. If there is a Bible or other material of a spiritual nature, if/when appropriate, encourage your students to engage their patient regarding their faith and current illness. For example, I recently cared for a patient who had a Bible in his room. I asked, *"Do you have a favorite passage, and if so would you like me to read it to you?"* He wanted me to read the Twenty-Third Psalm: *"The Lord is my shepherd; I shall not want..."* He closed his eyes and appeared relaxed as I read this to him. He thanked me afterwards and asked if I would pray for him. After a short prayer he fell asleep. This took only a couple of minutes, but it clearly ministered and cared for his spirit.

Power of Presence

Acknowledging what is present in the environment highlights a principle that I have found to be true in nursing practice: it is the LITTLE things that the nurse does that are in reality the BIG things that make a difference. One of the BIG things includes the power of nurse presence. Most students are unaware that their physical presence while providing care can meet the emotional and even spiritual needs of each patient in their care. But what does it mean to be "present"? To be present means that the nurse is AVAILABLE and ACCESSIBLE and this is clearly communicated to the patient. Presence can also be defined as "being with" and "being there" for the purpose of meeting their needs in a time of need. Other ways to define or explain presence include caring, nurturance, empathy, physical closeness, and physical touch (Rex–Smith, 2007).

When truly present, the nurse experiences what the patient feels (Faas, 2004). This is also the essence of empathy applied to practice. Presence is a nursing intervention that can be used in situations where there is nothing more that can be done but BE THERE by being supportive, or physically close, offering a touch, or sitting in silence (Rex–Smith, 2007). Sitting quietly in times of need can communicate so much more than any words, even if it is for just a moment. This was what I did when I sat briefly and was "present" to the woman who had just suffered a miscarriage.

In contrast, a "non-present" nurse would be aloof, outside the situation, or preoccupied with other thoughts though physically present (Benner & Wrubel, 1989). This is the tension students will experience as novice nurses who are focused on the "tasks" to be done. They may not be able to recognize the importance to be "present" in a way that communicates caring. Students must be given the grace to grow and develop as a new nurse, knowing that they will initially be focused on tasks. As they develop greater proficiency and progress, they will be able to be intentionally present to their patients.

Presence is also a nursing intervention recognized by the Nursing Interventions Classifications (NIC). Specific NIC presence interventions can be taught to students:

- Demonstrate accepting attitude.
- Verbally communicate empathy or understanding of the patient's experience.
- Establish patient trust.
- Listen to the patient's concern.

- Touch the patient to express concern as appropriate.

- Remain physically present without expecting interactional responses (Cavendish et al., 2003).

References

Benner, P. (1984). *From novice to expert: Excellence and power in clinical nursing practice.* Upper Saddle River, NJ: Prentice Hall.

Benner, P. (2013). Teacher curiosity, passion, engagement and self-cultivation–Essential for transformative education. Retrieved from http://www.educatingnurses.com/articles/teacher-curiosity-passion-engagement-and-self-cultivation-essential-for-transformative-education/

Benner, P. & Wrubel, J. (1988). Caring comes first. *American Journal of Nursing, 88*(8), 1073–1075.

Benner, P. & Wrubel, J. (1989). *Primacy of caring: Stress and coping in health and illness.* Menlo Park, CA: Addison-Wesley Publishing Company.

Benner, P., Hooper-Kyriakidis, P., & Stannard, D. (2011). *Clinical wisdom and interventions in acute and critical care: A thinking-in-action approach.* (2nd ed.). New York, NY: Springer.

Cavendish, R., Konecny, L., Mitzeliotis, C., Russo, D., Kraynyak Luise, B., Lanza, M., et al. (2003). Spiritual care activities of nurses using nursing interventions classifications (NIC) labels. *International Journal of Nursing Terminology Classifications, 16,* 120–121.

Faas, A. I. (2004). The intimacy of dying: An act of presence. *Dimensions of Critical Care Nursing, 23*(1), 76–78.

Leininger, M. (1988). Leininger's theory of nursing: Cultural care diversity and university. *Nursing Science Quarterly, 1,* 152–160.

Leininger, M. (1991). *Culture care diversity and universality: A theory of nursing.* New York, NY: National League for Nursing.

Murphy, L. S., & Walker, M. S. (2013). Spirit-guided care: Christian nursing for the whole person. *Journal of Christian Nursing, 30*(3), 144–152.

Orlick, S. & Benner, P. (1988). The primacy of caring. *American Journal of Nursing, 88*(3). 318–319.

Rex-Smith, A. (2007). Something more than presence. *Journal of Christian Nursing, 24*(2), 82–87.

Swanson, K. M. (1991). Empirical development of a middle range theory of caring. *Nursing Research, 40*(3), 161–166.

Swanson, K. M. (1999). *What is known about caring in nursing: A literary meta-analysis.* In A.S. Hinshaw, S.L. Feetham, & J.L.F. Shaver, eds. *Handbook of clinical nursing research.* Thousand Oaks, CA: Sage Publications.

PATIENT Dilemma

Pain Control or Drug Seeking Behavior

STUDENT Worksheet

Angela Stevens, 28 years old

Overview

Is pain always what the patient says it is? Though the patient's rating of pain is always relevant, the nurse must collect and cluster additional clinical data to make correct clinical judgments regarding pain control. In this dilemma, a post-operative patient with a history of narcotic tolerance and chemical dependency continues to require increasing amounts of narcotics for pain control. How to guide clinical decision making without being judgmental is the essence of this patient dilemma.

Clinical Dilemma Activity: STUDENT

Pain Control or Drug Seeking Behavior

I. Scenario

History of Present Problem:

Angela Stevens is a 28-year-old woman who is post-operative day (POD) #2 after a small bowel resection and lysis of adhesions. She has chronic abdominal pain due to severe Crohn's Disease and has developed narcotic tolerance and dependence as a result. She has been clinically stable post-op, but has been c/o increasing incisional pain despite the Fentanyl/Ropivicaine epidural drip being increased from 8 mL/hr to 12 mL/hr earlier today. She has hydromorphone (Dilaudid) 1mg IV push prn every 3 hours for abdominal pain that remains persistently greater than 6/10 on a 0-10 pain scale. Her pain goal is to be 4 or less.

Personal/Social History:

Angela is a single mother of two children ages three and one. She lives in her own apartment. She has struggled with chemical dependency in the past and denies any current problems. A routine urine drug screen before surgery was positive for benzodiazepines, even though she has no scheduled medications in this pharmacologic classification. She is estranged from her mother and has little support at home.

What data from the histories is important & RELEVANT; therefore it has clinical significance to the nurse?

RELEVANT Data from Present Problem:	Clinical Significance:
RELEVANT Data from Social History:	**Clinical Significance:**

II. The Dilemma Begins…

Current Concern:

It is now POD #4 and the epidural drip was discontinued earlier today. She has been watching the clock and calls the nurse precisely every three hours when she can have her next dose of hydromorphone 1 mg IV push prn. Despite her high level of pain that she consistently rates as an eight, her heart rate is 70, and her blood pressure is 110/68. When the nurse observes the patient discreetly through a window, Angela is texting on her phone and appears in no acute distress. As soon as the nurse enters the room, she puts the phone down and begins to moan loudly because of her pain.

What data from the current concern is important & RELEVANT; therefore it has clinical significance to the nurse?

RELEVANT Data from Current Concern:	Clinical Significance:

III. Resolving the Dilemma

1. *Identifying data that is RELEVANT, what is the essence of this current dilemma?*

2. *What additional information is needed by the nurse that would help clarify the current dilemma?*

3. *What additional members of the healthcare team could be used in this situation? Why?*

4. *What is the nursing priority?*

5. *What nursing interventions and/or principles can the nurse use to successfully resolve this clinical dilemma?*

6. *What is the expected response of the patient that indicate the nursing interventions were effective?*

7. *What response by the patient would indicate that a change in the plan of care and nursing interventions are needed?*

8. *What is the patient likely experiencing/feeling right now in this situation?*

9. *What can I do to engage myself with this patient's experience, and show that she matters to me as a person?*

10. *What was learned from this case study that you will incorporate into your practice?*

PATIENT Dilemma

Pain Control or Drug Seeking Behavior

Angela Stevens, 28 years old

Answer Key

Pain Control or Drug Seeking Behavior
I. Scenario
History of Present Problem:
Angela Stevens is a 28-year-old woman who is post-operative day (POD) #2 after a small bowel resection and lysis of adhesions. She has chronic abdominal pain due to severe Crohn's Disease and has developed narcotic tolerance and dependence as a result. She has been clinically stable post-op, but has been c/o increasing incisional pain despite the Fentanyl/Ropivicaine epidural drip being increased from 8 mL/hr to 12 mL/hr earlier today. She has hydromorphone (Dilaudid) 1mg IV push prn every 3 hours for abdominal pain that remains persistently greater than 6/10 on a 0-10 pain scale. Her pain goal is to be 4 or less.

Personal/Social History:
Angela is a single mother of two children ages three and one. She lives in her own apartment. She has struggled with chemical dependency in the past and denies any current problems. A routine urine drug screen before surgery was positive for benzodiazepines, even though she has no scheduled medications in this pharmacologic classification. She is estranged from her mother and has little support at home.

What data from the histories is important & RELEVANT; therefore it has clinical significance to the nurse?

RELEVANT Data from Present Problem:	Clinical Significance:
28-year-old woman who is post-operative day (POD) #2 after a small bowel resection and lysis of adhesions.	*It is ALWAYS relevant to note the age of the patient and determine if they are a higher risk for complications because of their age. Of the five rights of clinical reasoning, the "right" patient must always be considered as one who may be at higher risk for an adverse outcome because of age or other factors such as altered immune status or chronic illnesses (Levett–Jones et al., 2010).*
She has chronic abdominal pain due to severe Crohn's Disease and has developed narcotic tolerance and dependence as a result.	*Though Angela is young at only 28, she has a chronic illness with physiologic complications requiring surgery. Having a DEEP understanding of pathophysiology, a student would recognize that Crohn's Disease is a chronic inflammatory condition of the intestinal tract. What would be a common medication that is given to decrease inflammation that Angela is likely receiving?*
	Prednisone.
	How does prednisone impact the immune system? Angela is at a higher than expected risk for post-operative complications because prednisone impairs immunity. This is an excellent example of the essence of clinical reasoning that a nurse must demonstrate in practice!
	Because of the chronic abdominal pain that is typical with Crohn's Disease, and the amount of narcotics required to control the pain, narcotic tolerance and dependence develops. This is true for any patient with a chronic pain condition who is receiving narcotics.
	Take time to compare and contrast narcotic tolerance as well as narcotic dependence with your students to ensure that they understand the difference.
She has been clinically stable post-op, but has been c/o increasing incisional pain despite the Fentanyl/Ropivicaine epidural gtt being increased from 8 mL/hr to 12 mL/hr earlier today.	*It is challenging to manage post-operative pain in patients who have chronic pain and narcotic dependence and tolerance. Because of narcotic tolerance, they require higher amounts of narcotic pain medications to obtain pain relief in comparison to those who are opiate naïve. This is an essential piece of clinical data that the nurse MUST note for every patient that they are giving narcotics to for pain relief.*

	Knowing this will influence the dosage ranges that many prn medications have ordered.
	This need for an increase in the epidural drip is not unexpected, knowing that she has narcotic tolerance. The response to this must be noted. If this dosage remains ineffective, the CRNA or anesthesiologist will need to be notified to determine range for infusion rate.
She has hydromorphone (Dilaudid) 1mg IV push prn every 3 hours for abdominal pain that remains persistently greater than 6/10 on a 0-10 pain scale. Her pain goal is to be 4 or less.	*Though a patient is receiving an epidural drip, it is not uncommon to have additional systemic narcotics for additional pain control. Epidural is an excellent modality to control pain because the fentanyl is a very small dose deposited in the epidural space compared to what would be received if Angela received this intravenously. Therefore, the epidural medications have fewer systemic side effects.*
	The dosage of hydromorphone must be noted as HIGH but within range. This is expected because of her narcotic tolerance.
	Just because Angela has narcotic tolerance does not mean that she will not be impacted by too much narcotic medications. Remind students to closely assess for EARLY side effects of narcotic over-sedation that include confusion and altered level of consciousness/sedation. Respiratory depression is a LATE side effect. I find that my nursing students tend to focus on respiratory depression and the respiratory rate to the exclusion of all else.
RELEVANT Data from Social History:	**Clinical Significance:**
Angela is a single mother of two children ages three and one. She lives in her own apartment. She has struggled with chemical dependency in the past and denies any current problems.	*Angela is a single mother with young children who are completely dependent on her for care. The nurse needs to consider that Angela takes narcotics for chronic pain, which may have potential to impact her ability to care for two small children. Angela's chemical dependency history must be noted, but it is imperative NOT to make assumptions and judge her for this.*
A routine urine drug screen before surgery was positive for benzodiazepines, even though she has no scheduled medications in this pharmacologic classification.	*This is a problem!* *In order to fully recognize the severity of this piece of clinical data, the nurse must possess a DEEP understanding of pharmacology. What is the interaction between opiates and benzodiazepines? They exacerbate one another and together can cause lasting and prolonged sedation. This is why part of the instruction given to patients who are taking narcotics is to avoid ETOH because of the synergistic effects with a CNS depressant which is also what benzodiazepines produce. The most common benzodiazepines are lorazepam and diazepam.*
	Because Angela is a single mother, the implications of her misuse of benzodiazepines not only affect Angela, but also her two young children. It is imperative that the nurse takes the initiative to advocate for these children and follow protocol to contact child protection.
She is estranged from her mother and has little support at home.	*This is another psychosocial RED FLAG that must be noted by the nurse. This is especially concerning when combined with the knowledge of her use of benzodiazepines and the lack of any additional oversight or responsibility regarding the well-being of her children.*
	ISOLATION is a characteristic of those who are living an addictive

	lifestyle. Though the chart states that there are no current chemical dependency concerns, this finding is a RED FLAG and needs further evaluation.

II. The Dilemma Begins...

Current Concern:

It is now POD #4 and the epidural drip was discontinued earlier today. Angela has been watching the clock and calls the nurse precisely every three hours when she can have her next dose of hydromorphone 1 mg IV push prn. Despite her high level of pain that she consistently rates as an eight, her heart rate is 70, and her blood pressure is 110/68. When the nurse observes the patient discreetly through a window, Angela is texting on her phone and appears in no acute distress. As soon as the nurse enters the room, she puts the phone down and begins to moan loudly because of her pain.

What data from the current concern is important & RELEVANT; therefore it has clinical significance to the nurse?

RELEVANT Data from Current Concern:	Clinical Significance:
It is now POD #4 and the epidural drip was discontinued earlier today.	*Knowing that the epidural drip was discontinued is relevant, BUT she is also POD #4 and the amount of pain that is physiologically present should be DECREASING. The amount of medication to control pain would be expected to overall be LESS even though she has a narcotic tolerance.*
She has been watching the clock and calls the nurse precisely every three hours when she can have her next dose of hydromorphone 1 mg IV push prn.	*This by itself is NOT a RED FLAG for potential drug seeking behavior. If someone is in ongoing pain, knowing when the next dose is due is a typical response. By itself, it does NOT mean a patient may be drug-seeking.*
Despite her high level of pain that she consistently rates as an eight, her heart rate is 70, and her blood pressure is 110/68.	*One of the filters that a nurse must use in practice (as well as for the NCLEX) is to examine a clinical situation and determine if the clinical data that has been collected is EXPECTED or UNEXPECTED based on the nurse's knowledge of the applied sciences and clinical experience. What would be EXPECTED physiologically with a patient in severe levels of pain is an elevation in BP and/or heart rate. Both of these values are on the low side of normal and clearly not elevated. Patients with chronic pain do NOT always have the same physiologic response as those with acute pain with no chronic pain overlay so this is not always conclusive. However, this data needs to be clustered with what has been collected so far.* *Though it is commonly taught that a patient's pain is whatever they say it is, from my perspective, this approach to pain management in our culture has had a boomerang consequence that contributes to the record number of narcotic prescriptions for pain as well as inappropriate use of prescribed opiates. Therefore, it is imperative that, in addition to determining the level of pain a patient may have, the nurse does NOT stop collecting and clustering additional clinical data regarding a patient in pain to make a clinical judgment.*
When the nurse observes the patient discreetly through a window, Angela is texting on her phone and appears in no acute distress. As soon as the nurse enters the room, she puts the phone down and begins to moan loudly because of her pain.	*This is a RED FLAG that cannot be disregarded by the nurse. When a patient's behavior dramatically changes the moment that the nurse is present, in my clinical experience, this is typically seen in patients who are acting in a manner to receive narcotics in a drug-seeking manner.*

III. Resolving the Dilemma

1. Identifying data that is RELEVANT, what is the essence of this current dilemma?
There are two components to this dilemma:
1. The concern over the well-being of Angela's children over the potential abuse of benzodiazepines and the need to initiate a child protection referral to conclusively determine if this is a problem.
2. Misuse of pain medications while Angela is in the hospital that may indicate drug-seeking behavior or addiction.

2. What additional information is needed by the nurse that would help clarify the current dilemma?
- The concern over the well-being of Angela's children over the potential abuse of benzodiazepines and the need to initiate a child protection referral to conclusively determine if this is a problem.
  - Though a referral will need to be initiated regardless, it would be important to allow Angela to provide a rationale or explanation for the benzodiazepines in her urine.

- Misuse of pain medications while Angela is in the hospital that may indicate drug-seeking behavior
  - Clarification of what has been directly assessed and observed is appropriate for the nurse. Though it is important for the nurse to communicate what has been observed to the physician to determine an appropriate plan of care, if the nurse is comfortable doing so, he or she can communicate the observed behavior to the patient and allow the patient to provide an explanation.

3. What additional members of the healthcare team could be used in this situation? Why?
- **Primary care provider.** I have seen in the ED that some care providers will directly confront what is apparent drug-seeking behavior and establish clear boundaries of how a patient's pain will be managed and what they will receive in a prescription (narcotic or non-narcotic medication). This communication is best done by the primary care provider and not the nurse because doctors write the prescriptions, not the staff nurse!
- **Social services.** Though the referral for child protection will go to the county social services, since Angela is a patient in the hospital, the hospital social worker needs to be kept in the loop and can facilitate needed coordination between the two agencies.

4. What is the nursing priority?
Textbook learning is linear, with only topic presented at a time. Real-world practice can have multiple overlays that present at the same time that include physiologic as well as psychosocial problems. To have two relevant psychosocial problems with the same patient that need to be addressed is not that unusual.
Therefore I will address a nursing priority for each of the separate problems that are the essence of this situation:
- **Safety for the two children who may be experiencing neglect**
  - There is no NANDA nursing diagnostic statement that fits so simply stating the essence of the nursing priority which is to contact county child protection services to provide an assessment referral will suffice.

- **Misuse of pain medications that may indicate drug-seeking behavior**
  - Though acute/chronic pain would be the physiologic nursing priority that may still be relevant, the essence of the likelihood of drug-seeking behavior would make the NANDA nursing diagnostic statement "ineffective coping" as one possible motivation to pursue this behavior.

5. What nursing interventions and/or principles can the nurse use to successfully resolve this clinical dilemma?
- **Safety for the two children who may be experiencing neglect**
  - Simple...call child protection services in the county of record to initiate a referral/assessment.

- **Misuse of pain medications that may indicate drug-seeking behavior**
  - Notify the primary care provider of your concern.
  - AVOID ASSUMPTIONS. One of the essential caring interventions that Kristen Swanson (1991) identified in her research on caring was the importance of nurses making judgments or assuming things that may or may not be true regarding the patients under their care. As soon as the nurse makes an assumption, he/she ceases to be caring. It is imperative to use the standard of proof that is present in our legal system, innocent until proven guilty beyond a reasonable doubt. Just because you, as a nurse, do not struggle with addictive

behaviors that may be present with Angela, that does not make you a better person or give you a reason to look down on her. Continue to support and manage pain with a nonjudgmental attitude.

○ *Continue to collect all relevant data regarding pain control.*

6. What is the expected response of the patient that indicate the nursing interventions were effective?

Though issues regarding drug seeking behavior are not easily resolved because the motivating factors that drive this are related to addiction, it will not be until Angela has any insight into her behavior that there will be an ability to resolve this conflict satisfactorily. The first step of Alcoholics Anonymous that is used by other 12-step programs is acknowledging that she was "powerless and that her life has become unmanageable." Assessing for statements that represent these themes would indicate that she may be ready to consider treatment.

7. What response by the patient would indicate that a change in the plan of care and nursing interventions are needed?

If the patient becomes angry, hostile and excessively defensive when concerns over the presence of benzodiazepines in her urine and change of behavior with pain are presented, this would clearly demonstrate that Angela remains in some state of denial regarding her chemical dependency issues.

8. What is the patient likely experiencing/feeling right now in this situation?

Angela is likely fearful as well as anxious that her chemical use may be fully discovered and the consequences of her drug use and the custody of her children will be questioned..

9. What can I do to engage myself with this patient's experience, and show that she matters to me as a person?

It is essential that the nurse maintain a posture of empathy regarding Angela and her current concerns that support an ongoing struggle with addiction. Addicts pursue their addiction (ETOH/drugs/pornography/sexual, etc.) as a means to escape reality because to live with the emotional or spiritual pain that is present makes it a battle to live each day. Addiction provides a short-lived means of escape..

The nurse must be able to get into this patient's experience and NOT be judgmental over his past choices. This is essential and not optional. I have seen repeatedly how harsh and judgmental nurses can be with their patients in this context. We must remember the wisdom of Jesus when the woman caught in adultery was brought before him by the religious leaders. They asked Jesus whether or not she should be stoned. Jesus said, **"Let him who is without sin among you be the first to throw a stone at her."** *(John 8:3–11).*
None of us is better than an addict. The only difference is that some sins are easier hidden than others!

10. What was learned from this case study that you will incorporate into your practice?

Content knowledge without personal application will not be fruitful. Reflection is an essential professional behavior that can also be practiced! I have added this question to allow students to intentionally reflect on what they have learned so that they can integrate this essential content into their practice and fully develop the ethical comportment of the professional nurse. This question will facilitate rich dialogue in whatever context you choose to use this case study. If there is not enough time to discuss this question, consider having students write a one-page reflection paper.

References

Levett-Jones, T., Hoffman, K., Dempsey, J., Yeun-Sim Jeong, S., Noble, D., Norton, C. Hickey, N. (2010). The 'five rights' of clinical reasoning: An educational model to enhance nursing students' ability to identify and manage clinically 'at risk' patients. *Nurse Education Today, 30,* 515–520.

Swanson, K. M. (1991). Empirical development of a middle range theory of caring. *Nursing Research, 40*(3), 161–166.

PATIENT Dilemma

Anxiety or Spiritual Distress

STUDENT Worksheet

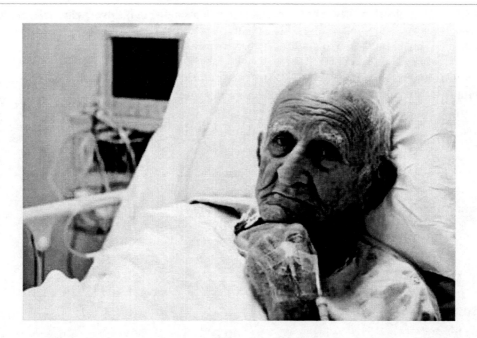

John James, 77 years old

Overview

When a patient is anxious, could this represent something more than a primary problem of anxiety? In this dilemma, a patient who almost died after surgery is making excellent progress, but something may be wrong. Does his sudden onset of shortness of breath and feelings of anxiety represent a physical, emotional, or a spiritual problem? The nurse needs to think in action and determine the current nursing priority to provide needed care and support.

Clinical Dilemma Activity: STUDENT
Anxiety or Spiritual Distress
I. Scenario
History of Present Problem:
John James is a 77-year-old man who had coronary artery bypass graft (CABG) x 4 vessels three days ago for multi-vessel coronary artery disease. He lost over 1000 mL of blood shortly after surgery due to a bleeding graft site and almost died as a result. He is currently off all vaso-active drips, his arterial line has been discontinued and he is clinically stable. John is scheduled to transfer to the cardiac step-down unit later today.

Personal/Social History:
John's wife died six months ago after fifty years of marriage. He lives alone in his own apartment. He has one son who lives in the area and checks in at least once a week to see how he is doing. He is a Vietnam War veteran who has not been active in his church since he returned from the war over forty years ago.

What data from the histories is important & RELEVANT; therefore it has clinical significance to the nurse?

RELEVANT Data from Present Problem:	Clinical Significance:
RELEVANT Data from Social History:	**Clinical Significance:**

II. The Dilemma Begins...
Current Concern:
John puts on his call light and as you enter the room he states that he feels short of breath and is visibly anxious. His breath sounds are clear and his O2 saturation is 98% on 2 liters n/c. His respiratory rate is 20/minute and his heart rate is 78/minute-sinus rhythm. He acknowledges that he is anxious and feels like he is having a panic attack and has never felt like this before. When you ask him if there is anything that he may be anxious about, he shares the following, "I used to go to church when I was little, but when I saw so many of my friends die in Vietnam and was helpless to save them, how could I believe in a God who allowed such horrible things to happen. Before the war I could not even kill a cat or dog. In Vietnam I killed so many people. How can I be forgiven for what I have done?"

What data from the current concern is important & RELEVANT; therefore it has clinical significance to the nurse?

RELEVANT Data from Current Concern:	Clinical Significance:

III. Resolving the Dilemma

1. Identifying data that is RELEVANT, what is the essence of this current dilemma?

2. What additional information is needed by the nurse that would help clarify the current dilemma?

3. What additional members of the healthcare team could be used in this situation? Why?

4. What is the nursing priority?

5. What nursing interventions and/or principles can the nurse use to successfully resolve this clinical dilemma?

6. What is the expected response of the patient that indicate the nursing interventions were effective?

7. What response by the patient would indicate that a change in the plan of care and nursing interventions are needed?

8. What is the patient likely experiencing/feeling right now in this situation?

9. What can I do to engage myself with this patient's experience, and show that he matters to me as a person?

10. What was learned from this case study that you will incorporate into your practice?

PATIENT Dilemma

Anxiety or Spiritual Distress

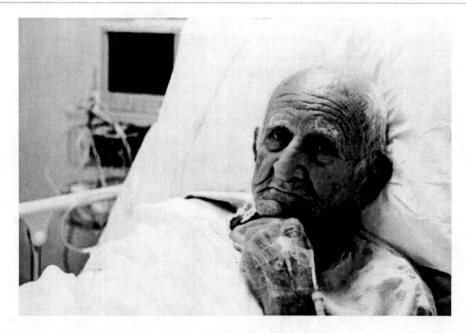

John James, 77 years old

Answer Key

Anxiety or Spiritual Distress

I. Scenario

History of Present Problem:

John James is a 77-year-old man who had coronary artery bypass graft (CABG) x 4 vessels three days ago for multi-vessel coronary artery disease. He lost over 1000 mL of blood shortly after surgery due to a bleeding graft site and almost died as a result. He is currently off all vaso-active drips, his arterial line has been discontinued and he is clinically stable. John is scheduled to transfer to the cardiac step-down unit later today.

Personal/Social History:

John's wife died six months ago after fifty years of marriage. He lives alone in his own apartment. He has one son who lives in the area and checks in at least once a week to see how he is doing. He is a Vietnam War veteran who has not been active in his church since he returned from the war over forty years ago.

What data from the histories is important & RELEVANT; therefore it has clinical significance to the nurse?

RELEVANT Data from Present Problem:	Clinical Significance:
He lost over 1000 mL of blood shortly after surgery due to a bleeding graft site and almost died as a result.	*The volume of blood loss is clinically significant. That he had a near-death experience as a result will likely result in psychosocial implications that must be noted by the nurse.*
He is currently off all vaso-active drips, his arterial line has been discontinued and he is clinically stable. John is scheduled to transfer to the cardiac step-down unit later today.	*This cluster of data makes it clear that although he had a critical event, he is currently clinically stable and there are no physiologic red flags regarding his physical status.*

RELEVANT Data from Social History:	Clinical Significance:
John's wife died six months ago after fifty years of marriage. He lives alone in his own apartment.	*The death of a spouse is one of the most significant psychosocial stressors that a person will experience. This loss was recent. That he is living alone after 50 years of marriage is another psychosocial piece of data that must be noted by the nurse.*
He has one son who lives in the area and checks in at least once a week to see how he is doing.	*Though he is alone, it is important to note that he does have family involvement in his care.*
He is a Vietnam War veteran who has not been active in his church since he returned from the war over forty years ago.	*Though the chart does not suggest a reason why he has not been active in his church, any combat war veteran will likely have some psychosocial distress or PTSD as a result. This is true especially if they have seen active combat.*

II. The Dilemma Begins…

Current Concern:

John puts on his call light and as you enter the room, he states that he feels short of breath and is visibly anxious. His breath sounds are clear and his O2 saturation is 98% on 2 liters n/c. His respiratory rate is 20/minute and his heart rate is 78/minute-sinus rhythm. He acknowledges that he is anxious and feels like he is having a panic attack. He has never felt like this before. When you ask him if there is anything that he may be anxious about, he shares the following, "I used to go to church when I was little, but when I saw so many of my friends die in Vietnam and was helpless to save them, how could I believe in a God who allowed such horrible things to happen? Before the war I could not even kill a cat or dog. In Vietnam I killed so many people. How can I be forgiven for what I have done?"

What data from the current concern is important & RELEVANT; therefore it has clinical significance to the nurse?

RELEVANT Data from Current Concern:	Clinical Significance:
He states that he feels short of breath and is visibly anxious.	*This data must be taken at face value as a physiologic concern and a possible complication that can represent a pulmonary embolus because of his recent surgery. The nurse must conduct a thorough assessment to determine if this is a possible problem.*
His breath sounds are clear and his O2 saturation is 98% on 2 liters n/c. His respiratory rate is 20/minute and his heart rate is 78/minute-sinus rhythm.	*This cluster of clinical data does not suggest a physiologic problem. The nurse would expect to see an elevated heart rate and elevated respiratory rate with a chief complaint of shortness of breath. Though a physiologic problem still needs to be considered, the nurse must also consider the more likely possibility of anxiety as the primary problem.*
He acknowledges that he is anxious and feels like he is having a panic attack and has never felt like this before.	*This statement by the patient makes it apparent that this problem of shortness of breath is more likely related to anxiety and not a physiologic problem. Therefore, the nurse must explore and ask an open-ended question to determine the cause of his anxiety.*
When you ask him if there is anything that he may be anxious about, he shares the following, "I used to go to church when I was little, but when I saw so many of my friends die in Vietnam and was helpless to save them, how could I believe in a God who allowed such horrible things to happen. Before the war I could not even kill a cat or dog. In Vietnam I killed so many people. How can I be forgiven for what I have done..."	*This admission is extremely significant as well as tragic. The relationship of this clinical data, when combined with the near-death experience, is a psychosocial as well as spiritual concern. The primary problem is more than just anxiety but spiritual distress. He clearly is in despair and looking for forgiveness. This reflection is not uncommon for patients who are dying or are facing the possibility of an adverse outcome based on their current problem. The nurse must be prepared to respond in a caring, therapeutic, and empathetic manner that will provide support, especially when a chaplain is nowhere to be found!*

III. Resolving the Dilemma

1. Identifying data that is RELEVANT, what is the essence of this current dilemma?
Though NANDA nursing diagnostic statements do not always capture the essence of a patient care priority, in this scenario, spiritual distress captures the essence of what the nurse is encountering in this scenario.

2. What additional information is needed by the nurse that would help clarify the current dilemma?
The patient has already disclosed an adequate amount of information based on his combat experiences in Vietnam. He has expressed a crisis in his belief in God as well as anger at God for not being able to save his friends. He also is expressing regret over the human beings he killed in combat and a need for forgiveness that he has not been able to experience. To obtain additional information to clarify spiritual needs or assessment, here are some practical guidance for students:

How to practically assess spirituality at the end of life.
This patient is at the end of life and spiritual issues often surface at this point, though they may not be readily apparent. Spiritual assessment for this patient might be explored with the FICA acronym. This model is useful for any faith belief system. FICA acronym represents:

- *F-Faith or beliefs: What are your spiritual beliefs? Do you consider yourself spiritual? What things do you believe in that give meaning to life?*
- *I-Importance and influence: Is faith important to you? How has your illness or hospitalization affected your personal belief practices?*

- **C-Community:** *Are you connected to a faith center in the community? Does it provide support/comfort for you during times of stress? Is there a person/group who assists you in your spirituality?*
- **A-Address:** *What can I do for you? What support can health care provide to support your spiritual beliefs/practices? (Dameron, 2005).*

These questions would naturally explore this patient's spirituality. It is always best if the nurse has some comfort with the exploration of spirituality. Patients can sense discomfort or anxiety in approaching this portion of the assessment. The FICA model offers some open-ended questions to make spiritual assessment a natural part of the conversation. Use this spiritual assessment tool to make caring for the spirit an essential component of your nursing practice!

3. What additional members of the healthcare team could be used in this situation? Why?
A chaplain would be the most obvious and best outside resource. But with matters of faith and religion, the nurse must first obtain the patient's consent for a chaplain visit. If the patient does not want this visit, even though the nurse knows that it would likely have benefit, the autonomy of the patient must be respected and the referral should not be made.

4. What is the nursing priority?
Spiritual distress.
Identifying the essence of the patient scenario and correctly determining the nursing priority is a foundational aspect of clinical reasoning. In any clinical scenario, the nursing priority may or may NOT be a NANDA nursing diagnosis. The following NANDA nursing diagnostic statements capture the essence of this scenario include:
- *Hopelessness*
- *Grieving*
- *Ineffective coping*

5. What nursing interventions and/or principles can the nurse use to successfully resolve this clinical dilemma?

Nursing care for a patient in spiritual distress involves the following foundational aspects:

1. *A caring, nurse-patient relationship. Patients report that their distress was relieved when the nurse cared for them holistically, provided freedom of choice when possible, and when the nurse simply listened and gave the patient a chance to talk (Creel, 2007; Sellers, 2001).*
2. *Spirituality is a coping mechanism that can be used by patients to transcend their current illness and suffering and provide meaning (Emblem & Halstead, 1993).*
3. *Active listening and facilitating the patient's verbalization of concerns are foundational to spiritual care.*
4. *Nurses do not need to know about specific beliefs, religions or spiritual practices to provide effective spiritual care (Martin, Burrows and Pomillo, 1983).*
5. *Spiritual care involves communicating respect for the patient, listening and appropriate self-disclosure (Sellers, 2001; Taylor, 2003).*

The essence of spiritual care is providing hope when life appears hopeless. There are numerous caring interventions that the nurse can use to actively demonstrate support and care for this patient in a time of crisis. These interventions comprise the essence of the "art" of nursing and could include the following:

- *Respect and support the patient's faith and religious belief system by making appropriate referrals.*
- *Acknowledge the patient's suffering and act to ease suffering by showing compassion.*
- *Allow the patient to verbalize anger and fear.*
- *Help the patient deal with feelings of guilt and instill hope (Villagomeza, 2005).*

Additional principles that are foundational to spiritual care include:
Nurse presence.
When the nurse is present and with the patient in a non-hurried manner, this clearly communicates caring and support. Presence for the nurse is being present in the moment with the patient and his moment which is happening now. The emotional breakthroughs don't last long, but are critical for nurses to connect with the patient. Patients sense whether

the nurse is willing to "go there" or not. If they sense you are not willing to be in the moment with them, they will pull back and the moment ends. If the nurse fiddles with the computer or indicates nonverbally a discomfort with what is happening, it will decrease trust in the nurse.

Patients don't care how much you know until they know how much you care. This is about focusing on the patient and giving caring responses to build trust. It truly is a privilege for the nurse to have a patient share the "tough stuff" in life with you. Generally, the patient will not share like this unless they trust you or they are in an affective domain crisis. This patient is in crisis of belief and ready for a breakthrough moment. The question is, will the nurse be willing to go there with him?

Silence. It is important to recognize that there are situations where no words are needed. Sitting in silence with a patient in this context does not need to be awkward but indirectly communicates presence as well as caring. Pauses can be productive. They allow patients to process what is happening to them. After the silence, be willing to listen and go where the patient takes you.

Touch.
Reaching out and touching the patient's hand or shoulder and assessing the response to this intervention also communicates caring and support in this scenario.

Open-ended spiritual assessment questions.
There are a number of questions that the nurse can ask a patient in spiritual crisis. At times, asking one question will open up the conversation and the patient will begin to share openly.
  o Are you connected with a faith community?
  o What is your source of strength, peace, faith, hope, and worth?
  o What spiritual practices are important to you?
  o What can I do to support your faith?

Though each of these questions are effective tools to make a quick spiritual assessment for most patients, in this scenario most of these questions are not relevant because John does not have a faith community that he identifies with. But there is one question that should be considered: What is your source of strength or peace? He may have some personal strategies or approaches that he has drawn upon in the past.

Prayer.
Just as there are moments where nothing can be said, there are times where it is equally apparent that the most effective and appropriate nursing intervention is to pray. To do this, the nurse must recognize the value of faith and spirituality in his/her own life and have something to offer and give.

My faith is an essential component of who I am. I am comfortable addressing matters of the spirit when they arise in caring for others. Do not underestimate the power of prayer and the comfort it can provide to patients. I have yet to have a patient decline an offer for prayer when I sensed it was appropriate to go there.

A response I frequently use is, "God is waiting for you. He cares about you."

The follow-up could be "Would you like me to pray with you?"

"How would you like me to pray?" Only if the nurse is comfortable with prayer, pray with the patient. JACHO recognizes that it is ok for nurses to pray with patients as long as they have permission from the patient and are attentive to pray in a way that is meaningful to the patient.

In my practice, when I ask a patient about their source of strength and hope, after they have answered, they will sometimes turn the question back to me and ask what is MY source of strength and hope? If the nurse has a faith tradition that is meaningful and relevant to them and if the nurse is comfortable sharing, it is appropriate to share and assess the patient's response. If the patient begins to inquire and ask questions of religion and faith to the nurse, it is not inappropriate or proselytizing to share your faith in response. This must be done carefully and respectfully. As long as the patient is initiating the dialogue and the nurse remains patient-centered in what is disclosed, this sharing and disclosure can benefit and comfort the patient who clearly is in spiritual distress.

Pitfalls to avoid in addressing issues of spiritual distress include:

- *Trying to solve the patient's problems or resolve unanswerable questions.*
- *Going beyond the nurse's role or expertise or imposing personal spiritual beliefs on the patient.*
- *Providing premature reassurance to the patient (Lo, B. et al., 2002).*

6. What is the expected response of the patient that indicate that the nursing interventions were effective?
Because the patient is clearly anxious and even has the physiologic complaint of shortness of breath, the alleviation of shortness of breath, and relaxed affect would be the most obvious assessment findings that the nursing interventions of caring, empathy, and support were effective.

7. What response by the patient would indicate that a change in the plan of care and nursing interventions are needed?
If the patient continued to be visibly anxious, in distress, or short of breath, this would indicate that the support and care that was offered was not effective. It would be appropriate for the nurse to look at pharmacologic interventions such as lorazepam (Ativan) to decrease anxiety as needed if this is not ordered in the medication record.

8. What is the patient and family likely experiencing/feeling right now in this situation?
John's experience of spiritual distress is clearly evident. What is not known is how his John's son is processing this current situation. If he come to visit, it would be appropriate to clarify how he is doing and answer any questions he may have.

9. What can I do to engage myself with this patient's experience, and show that he matters to me as a person?
The essence of empathy is to put oneself in the shoes of those you are caring for or the family and how they are responding. If the nurse can consciously make this transition, it becomes much easier to be moved with a heart of compassion for those that one cares for.

Swanson (1991) identified the following caring interventions in the practice setting that have relevance in this scenario to engage with this patient's experience and support both the patient and family in this crisis:

Family caring interventions
- *Maintain a hope-filled attitude*
- *Offer realistic optimism*
- *Support the family*
- *Explain all that is taking place and answer any/all questions*
- *Convey availability to the family*

Patient caring interventions
- *Preserve the dignity of the patient*
- *Anticipate needs*
- *Comfort the patient in any way*
- *Seek cues by paying close attention to the patient's response and anticipate her expected response*
- *Perform competently and skillfully as a nurse. This communicates caring to your patient!*
- *Convey availability to the patient*

10. What was learned from this case study that you will incorporate into your practice?
Content knowledge without personal application will not be fruitful. Reflection is an essential professional behavior that can also be practiced! I have added this question to allow students to intentionally reflect on what they have learned so that they can integrate this essential content into their practice and fully develop the ethical comportment of the professional nurse. This question will facilitate rich dialogue in whatever context you choose to use this case study. If there is not enough time to discuss this question, consider having students write a one-page reflection paper.

References

Creel, E. (2007). The meaning of spiritual nursing acre for ill individuals with no religious affiliation. *International Journal for Human Caring* 11(3): 14-21.

Dameron, C.M. (2005). Spiritual assessment made easy…With acronyms! *Journal of Christian Nursing*, 22, 14-16.

Emblem, J. D. & Halstead, L. (1993). Spiritual needs and interventions: Comparing the views of patients, nurses and chaplains. *Clinical Nurse Specialist* 7(4): 175-182.

Gulanick, M. , Myers, J., Klopp, A., et al. (2003) *Nursing Care Plans: Nursing Diagnosis and Intervention.* 5th ed. St. Louis: Mosby

Lo, B., Ruston, D., Kates, L.W. et al. (2002). Discussing religious and spiritual issues at the end of life: A practical guide for physicians. *Journal of the American Medical Association.* 287(6): 749-754.

Martin, C., Burrows, C., & Pomilio, J. (1983). Spiritual needs of patients study. In Fish, S. & Shelly J. (Eds) *Spiritual care: The nurse's role.* Downer's Grove, IL: Intervarsity Press.

Sellers, S. (2001). The spiritual care meanings of adults residing in the Midwest. *Nursing Science Quarterly* 14 (3): 239-249.

Swanson, K. M. (1991). Empirical development of a middle range theory of caring. *Nursing Research, 40*(3), 161–166.

Taylor, E.J. (2007) *What Do I Say? Talking with Patients about Spirituality.* Templeton Press: Philadelphia.

Villagomeza, L. R. (2005). Spiritual distress in adult cancer patients. *Holistic Nursing Practice.* November/December: 285-294.

PATIENT Dilemma

Depressed Patient/Loss of Hope

STUDENT Worksheet

Anne Shirley, 48 years old

Overview

Each patient responds differently to the stress of illness and the change of life that it represents. Though the patient's physical needs are the initial concern, over time, the emotional and even spiritual needs may become a priority. This scenario addresses this dilemma and how the nurse can practically support and care for a patient who is depressed and has lost hope.

Depressed Patient/Loss of Hope

I. Scenario

History of Present Problem:

Anne Shirley is a previously healthy 48-year-old woman who has been hospitalized the past month for complications from an open hysterectomy. Anne became septic three days after surgery which then progressed to septic shock. She was emergently transferred to ICU where she required multiple vasopressors and intubation. Anne transferred out of ICU two days ago to the medical floor. She now requires dialysis three times a week due to acute tubular necrosis (ATN) that she experienced as a complication from septic shock. Her kidney function is not expected to recover. She is extremely weak and deconditioned due to her three weeks in ICU.

Personal/Social History:

Anne is married with two daughters who are both teenagers. Her husband is supportive, but overwhelmed by this unexpected medical crisis.

What data from the histories is important & RELEVANT; therefore it has clinical significance to the nurse?

RELEVANT Data from Present Problem:	Clinical Significance:

RELEVANT Data from Social History:	Clinical Significance:

II. The Dilemma Begins...

Current Concern:

Anne has a flat affect, and is visibly withdrawn. When the primary nurse enters the room she angrily states, "Just leave me alone, I don't want to do anything today! I am so done, I just want to die!" She turns away and begins to cry.

What data from the current concern is important & RELEVANT; therefore it has clinical significance to the nurse?

RELEVANT Data from Current Concern:	Clinical Significance:

III. Resolving the Dilemma

1. *Identifying data that is RELEVANT, what is the essence of this current dilemma?*

2. *What additional information is needed by the nurse that would help clarify the current dilemma?*

3. *What additional members of the healthcare team could be used in this situation? Why?*

4. *What is the nursing priority?*

5. *What nursing interventions and/or principles can the nurse use to successfully resolve this clinical dilemma?*

6. *What is the expected response of the patient that indicate the nursing interventions were effective?*

7. *What response by the patient would indicate that a change in the plan of care and nursing interventions are needed?*

8. *What is the patient and family likely experiencing/feeling right now in this situation?*

9. *What can I do to engage myself with this patient's experience, and show that she matters to me as a person?*

10. *What was learned from this case study that you will incorporate into your practice?*

PATIENT Dilemma

Depressed Patient/Loss of Hope

Anne Shirley, 48 years old

Answer Key

Clinical Dilemma Activity: ANSWER KEY

Depressed Patient/Loss of Hope

I. Scenario

History of Present Problem:

Anne Shirley is a previously healthy 48-year-old woman who has been hospitalized the past month for complications from an open hysterectomy. Anne became septic three days after surgery which then progressed to septic shock. She was emergently transferred to ICU where she required multiple vasopressors and intubation. Anne transferred out of ICU two days ago to the medical floor. She now requires dialysis three times a week due to acute tubular necrosis (ATN) that she experienced as a complication from septic shock. Her kidney function is not expected to recover. She is extremely weak and deconditioned due to her three weeks in ICU.

Personal/Social History:

Anne is married with two daughters who are both teenagers. Her husband is supportive, but overwhelmed by this unexpected medical crisis.

What data from the histories is important & RELEVANT; therefore it has clinical significance to the nurse?

RELEVANT Data from Present Problem:	Clinical Significance:
Previously healthy 48-year-old woman who has been hospitalized the past month for complications from an open hysterectomy.	*Is extremely important to note that this patient has been functioning at a very high level and has NOT been chronically ill despite her current presentation. The importance of nurse empathy, remembering that Anne was once a healthy individual who is now experiencing life-changing physiologic complications is an important first step that the nurse must undertake to provide a context of genuine caring and compassion for this patient.*
Anne became septic three days after surgery which then progressed to septic shock. She was emergently transferred to ICU where she required multiple vasopressors and intubation.	*No surgery is without risk and sepsis is the most common complication nurses will experience in clinical practice. If sepsis is allowed to progress to septic shock, the physiologic complications can be devastating as well as life-threatening. Though any surgical patient may appear clinically stable, it is imperative that the nurse identifies and is vigilant in looking for EARLY signs of sepsis which include fever, tachycardia, and heart rate greater than 90, as well as a blood pressure reading that may be normal but is beginning to TREND downwards.*
Anne transferred out of ICU two days ago to the medical floor. She now requires dialysis three times a week due to acute tubular necrosis (ATN) that she experienced as a complication from septic shock. Her kidney function is not expected to recover.	*Because of the lack of perfusion to the kidneys resulting from the shock state of sepsis, acute tubular necrosis is a common complication that can result in either acute or chronic renal failure. Unfortunately for Anne, her kidney function will likely never recover. The implications of being on dialysis for the rest of your life for a patient who was previously healthy must not be underestimated by the nurse. Empathetic understanding is essential to lay a foundation of caring and compassion so that the nurse can handle any response by the patient who may be angry or say something that appears to be directed at the nurse when it is not.*
She is extremely weak and deconditioned due to her three weeks in ICU.	*Any patient who has been in critical care for any length of time undergoes significant deconditioning. Physical as well as occupational therapy is essential as well as early mobility. Though promoting activity is a little thing, in reality it is a BIG thing that this patient requires. As she slowly regains her physical strength, this tends to also help strengthen her emotional and the spiritual strength as well.*

RELEVANT Data from Social History:	Clinical Significance:
Anne is married with two daughters who are both teenagers.	It is important to note that Anne is married and has this support in her life. She also has two teenage daughters who likely depend on her for guidance and support in this phase of their life as adolescents. This is another consideration that may contribute to the amount of stress Anne is experiencing right now.
Her husband is supportive, but overwhelmed with this unexpected medical crisis.	Recognizing the need to support Anne's overwhelmed husband is an important observation by the nurse that is significant. It is essential to remember that the nurse does not care only is for the patient, but also the immediate family. Therefore, the support that is needed for the patient in this scenario must also be extended to the immediate family including the husband and daughters when they are present. Though the nurse is often extremely busy, having an awareness and sensitivity to the needs of the immediate family is also extremely important and must be on the nurse's radar.

II. The Dilemma Begins…

Current Concern:

Anne has a flat affect, and is visibly withdrawn. When the primary nurse enters the room she angrily states, "Just leave me alone, I don't want to do anything today! I am so done, I just want to die!" She turns away and begins to cry.

What data from the current concern is important & RELEVANT; therefore it has clinical significance to the nurse?

RELEVANT Data from Current Concern:	Clinical Significance:
Anne has a flat affect, and is visibly withdrawn.	In addition to paying close attention to what the patient says, it is just as important if not more to discern the nonverbal communication that a patient demonstrates. Nonverbal actions are an accurate reflection of how the patient really feels.
When the primary nurse enters the room she angrily states, "Just leave me alone, I don't want to do anything today! I am so done, I just want to die!"	This statement by the patient confirms what the nonverbal communication has demonstrated and most likely represents depression. This must be taken seriously. Additional support is likely needed. It is important that the nurse does not take this statement personally as an attack on her. It is more a reflection of all that Anne has experienced in the life-changing consequences of septic shock that progressed to end-stage renal failure.
She turns away and begins to cry.	She is obviously extremely upset, depressed. This presentation may also represent a spiritual crisis as well. Though this is not known at this time, it is something that the nurse must consider. Depression and its resultant lack of purpose or meaning can also present the essence of a spiritual crisis. Many patients who have experienced unexpected life changes will ask, "Why, God?" This response and what it represents will require further exploration by the nurse.

III. Resolving the Dilemma

1. Identifying data that is RELEVANT, what is the essence of this current dilemma?
It is evident that Anne is experiencing severe depression that may represent a spiritual crisis.

2. What additional information is needed by the nurse to help clarify the current dilemma?
The depression is evidenced in both the nonverbal and verbal communication. It is not clear if this also represents a spiritual crisis. Though the nurse may feel unprepared to explore the spiritual dimension to her patient's depression, it

would be appropriate for the nurse to ask if the patient would want a chaplain to visit her, recognizing the spiritual implications of her obvious anger and depression that this may represent.

These questions, if used in this scenario by the nurse, would naturally explore this patient's spirituality. It is always best if the nurse has some comfort with the exploration of spirituality. Patients can sense discomfort or anxiety in approaching this portion of the assessment. The FICA model offers some open-ended questions to make spiritual assessment a natural part of the conversation. Use this spiritual assessment tool to make caring for the spirit an essential component of your nursing practice!

- **F-Faith or beliefs:** *What are your spiritual beliefs? Do you consider yourself spiritual? What things do you believe in that give meaning to life?*
- **I-Importance and influence:** *Is faith important to you? How has your illness or hospitalization affected your personal belief practices?*
- **C-Community:** *Are you connected to a faith center in the community? Does it provide support/comfort for you during times of stress? Is there a person/group who assists you in your spirituality?*
- **A-Address:** *What can I do for you? What support can health care provide to support your spiritual beliefs/practices? (Dameron, 2005).*

3. What additional members of the healthcare team could be used in this situation? Why?
A chaplain would be the most obvious and best outside resource the nurse should attempt to use.. However, in matters of faith and religion, the nurse must first obtain the patient's consent for a chaplain visit. If the patient does not want this visit, even though the nurse knows that it would likely have benefit, the autonomy of the patient must be respected and the referral should not be made.

4. What is the nursing priority?
Though clinical reasoning represents identifying the essence of the nursing priority that may or may NOT be a NANDA nursing diagnosis, the following NANDA nursing diagnostic statements capture in varying degrees what the nursing priority represents:
- Ineffective coping
- Hopelessness
- Grieving
- Powerlessness
- Spiritual distress?

5. What nursing interventions and/or principles can the nurse use to successfully resolve this clinical dilemma?
The essence of spiritual care is providing hope when life appears hopeless. There are numerous caring interventions that the nurse can use to actively demonstrate support and care for this patient in a time of crisis and to provide hope and support. These interventions comprise the essence of the "art" of nursing and could include the following:
- **Nurse presence.** When the nurse is present and with the patient in a non-hurried manner, this clearly communicates caring and support that Anne needs at this time. It is imperative to NOT take her anger as a personal affront. It is NOT directed at the nurse personally, so it is especially important to maintain presence and not respond to the words but to the underlying MESSAGE of what she is feeling.

  Patients don't care how much you know until they know how much you care. This is about focusing on the patient and caring responses to build trust. Remaining present and addressing the underlying message behind what Anne is sayings will clearly communicate caring and will be the foundation to establish trust in this difficult situation.

  Listening carefully to the patient by determining the overall "message" of what is being communicated is an essential nursing intervention. Use the therapeutic communication skill of paraphrasing to communicate clearly to the patient that they have been "heard" by the nurse.

- **Silence.** It is important to recognize that there are situations where no words are needed. Sitting in silence with a patient in this context does not need to be awkward but indirectly communicates presence as well as caring which will support the patient in this crisis.

- **Touch.** *Reaching out and touching the patient's hand or shoulder and assessing the response to this intervention also communicates caring and support. One cannot know how a patient will receive touch so the nurse must first assess the patient response. If the nurse allows the patient in control to withdraw touch, it simplifies evaluation of the intervention of touch. One simple way to implement this approach is to slip your hand under the patient's hand with your palm up. The patient can withdraw their hand at any time if the nurse's hand is not on top of the patient's hand and provides needed control for the patient.*

- **Open ended spiritual assessment questions.** *There are a number of questions that the nurse can ask a patient who is depressed or may be in spiritual crisis:*
    - *Are you connected with a faith community?*
    - *What is your source of strength, peace, faith, hope, and worth?*
    - *What spiritual practices are important to you?*
    - *What can I do to support your faith?*
    - *What makes life meaningful for you?*
    - *What do you feel is the meaning of all this?*

Though these spiritual assessment questions are tools that the nurse can use to clarify spiritual needs and assessment, in this scenario the use of these questions would be appropriate only if the patient were to respond and talk with the nurse regarding what she feels and experiences in the present.

6. What is the expected response of the patient that indicate the nursing interventions were effective?
The response by the patient that would indicate that the nursing interventions were effective would include having the patient simply verbalize what she is feeling. Despite the emotional pain that many patients experience in depression, many do not want to verbalize what they are feeling. Therefore, to have the patient express her feelings in any way would be significant and would demonstrate that these nursing interventions were effective.

7. What response by the patient would indicate that a change in the plan of care and nursing interventions are needed?
Conversely, if the patient did not express any communication but remained silent and withdrawn, this would indicate that additional intervention and resources will likely be needed.

8. What is the patient and family likely experiencing/feeling right now in this situation?
Anne's experience is known, as well as her husband who is overwhelmed, but the needs of the two children are not known. If the husband and children come to visit, it is important that the nurse checks in with the children to see how they are processing this experience and answer any questions they may have to clarify their feelings and determine if additional or outside support is needed.

9. What can I do to engage myself with this patient's experience, and show that she matters to me as a person?
The essence of empathy is to put one's self in the shoes of those you are caring for or the family and how they are responding. If the nurse can consciously make this transition, it becomes much easier to be moved with a heart of compassion for those that one cares for.

Swanson (1991) identified the following caring interventions in the practice setting that have relevance in this scenario and to engage with this patient's experience, and support the patient and family in this crisis:

Family caring interventions
- *Maintain a hope-filled attitude*
- *Offer realistic optimism*
- *Support the family*
- *Explain all that is taking place and answer any/all questions*
- *Convey availability to the family*

Patient caring interventions
- *Preserve the dignity of the patient*
- *Anticipate needs*

- *Comfort the patient in any way*
- *Seek cues by paying close attention to the patient's response and anticipate her expected response*
- *Perform competently and skillfully as a nurse. This communicates caring to your patient!*
- *Convey availability to the patient*

10. What was learned from this case study that you will incorporate into your practice?
Content knowledge without personal application will not be fruitful. Reflection is an essential professional behavior that can also be practiced! I have added this question to allow students to intentionally reflect on what they have learned so that they can integrate this essential content into their practice and fully develop the ethical comportment of the professional nurse. This question will facilitate rich dialogue in whatever context you choose to use this case study. If there is not enough time to discuss this question, consider having students write a one-page reflection paper.

References

Swanson, K. M. (1991). Empirical development of a middle range theory of caring. *Nursing Research, 40*(3), 161–166.

PATIENT Dilemma

Chemotherapy/End of Life

STUDENT Worksheet

Ken Johnson, 52 years old

Overview

Holistic nursing care entails caring for not just the physical needs of every patient, but also the soul (emotional) and the spirit. In this dilemma, a patient with a stage IV lung cancer has a strong faith and belief system, but his illness is beginning to cause him to question his faith. How the nurse can practically support and care for his emotional and spiritual needs in this context is the essence of this patient dilemma.

Clinical Dilemma Activity: STUDENT

Chemotherapy/End of Life

I. Scenario

History of Present Problem:

Ken Johnson is a 52-year-old who was diagnosed with stage IV small cell lung cancer two years ago. He has been managed with a daily oral chemotherapeutic drug that had kept his tumors in both lung fields and lymph nodes in remission. He had a repeat CT scan last month that revealed that every tumor had grown dramatically in size and that he would need to undergo aggressive intravenous chemotherapy to have any hope of long-term survival.

Personal/Social History:

Ken has a strong Christian faith and acknowledges that he feels that God has used the numerous people who are praying for him as well as the medical care he has received have kept him alive. He has a supportive wife and two teenage sons.

What data from the histories is important & RELEVANT; therefore it has clinical significance to the nurse?

RELEVANT Data from Present Problem:	Clinical Significance:
RELEVANT Data from Social History:	**Clinical Significance:**

II. The Dilemma Begins…

Current Concern:

Ken comes to receive his second dose of intravenous chemotherapy. Instead of the optimistic attitude and bright affect he had last week, Ken is withdrawn and has a flat affect. When asked how he is doing, he replies, "The past three weeks have been so hard. I had no idea how painful chemo would be and how persistent the nausea and vomiting have been. I have no strength. I have been praying, other people have been praying for me and I thought I was going to be healed. I know God can heal and do the impossible. I have two sons who still need a father. Why has God chosen not to heal me? I don't know how long I can do this…"

What data from the current concern is important & RELEVANT; therefore it has clinical significance to the nurse?

RELEVANT Data from Current Concern:	Clinical Significance:

III. Resolving the Dilemma

1. Identifying data that is RELEVANT, what is the essence of this current dilemma?

2. What additional information is needed by the nurse that would help clarify the current dilemma?

3. What additional members of the healthcare team could be used in this situation? Why?

4. What is the nursing priority?

5. What nursing interventions and/or principles can the nurse use to successfully resolve this clinical dilemma?

6. What is the expected response of the patient that indicate the nursing interventions were effective?

7. What response by the patient would indicate that a change in the plan of care and nursing interventions are needed?

8. What is the patient or family likely experiencing/feeling right now in this situation?

9. What can I do to engage myself with this patient's experience, and show that he matters to me as a person?

10. What was learned from this case study that you will incorporate into your practice?

PATIENT Dilemma

Chemotherapy/End of Life

Ken Johnson, 52 years old

Answer Key

Chemotherapy/End of Life

I. Scenario

History of Present Problem:

Ken Johnson is a 52-year-old who was diagnosed with stage IV small cell lung cancer two years ago. He has been managed with a daily oral chemotherapeutic drug that had kept his tumors in both lung fields and lymph nodes in remission. He had a repeat CT scan last month that revealed that every tumor had grown dramatically in size and that he would need to undergo aggressive intravenous chemotherapy to have any hope of long-term survival.

Personal/Social History:

Ken has a strong Christian faith and acknowledges that he feels that God has used the numerous people who are praying for him as well as the medical care he has received have kept him alive. He has a supportive wife and two teenage sons.

What data from the histories is important & RELEVANT; therefore it has clinical significance to the nurse?

RELEVANT Data from Present Problem:	Clinical Significance:
52-year-old who was diagnosed with stage IV small cell lung cancer two years ago. He has been managed with a daily oral chemotherapeutic drug that had kept his tumors in both lung fields and lymph nodes in remission.	*Ken has terminal stage IV cancer which indicates that he has a primary tumor with metastasis. Small cell lung cancer must be recognized as an aggressive cancer that has one of the highest mortality rates of all cancers. Though his clinical picture remains guarded, his illness is being successfully managed by his current chemotherapy and is in remission. This is the best outcome that Ken could hope for under these circumstances.*
He had a repeat CT scan last month that revealed that every tumor had grown dramatically in size and that he would need to undergo aggressive intravenous chemotherapy to have any hope of long-term survival.	*Unfortunately, his clinical picture has quickly changed. The rapid growth of every tumor is a reflection of the aggressiveness of this type of cancer. Without an aggressive chemotherapy regimen, Ken will likely die in a short length of time.*
RELEVANT Data from Social History:	**Clinical Significance:**
Ken has a strong Christian faith and acknowledges that he feels that God has used the numerous people who are praying for him as well as the medical care he has received have kept him alive..	*Faith and the power of prayer have been shown to improve patient outcomes. Ken's faith is clearly important to him, therefore the nurse must have a sensitivity and awareness of his faith and do whatever is needed to support Ken and his family.*
	This principle is true regardless of the faith the patient or family may embrace. Though it is naturally easier to identify and support the faith of those patients who are similar to the nurse's, make it a priority to understand the tenets of other religions that are commonly seen in practice.
	For example, in Minneapolis, where I practice, there is a large Somalian immigrant group which is predominantly Muslim. Though this is not my faith tradition, I need to understand basic aspects of this culture and religion in order to better support patients and the family members who are Muslim.
	Another context that this principle applies is to nursing students who are atheist or agnostic. Just because a nurse does not adhere to a faith tradition of any kind does NOT give them a pass to make spiritual support less of a priority as they provide care. It is NOT about the nurse, but about the patient and their needs.

He has a supportive wife and two teenage sons.	*The presence of family psychosocial support must be noted by the nurse. Though this is a routine determination and assessment, it must not be taken for granted.*

II. The Dilemma Begins…

Current Concern:

Ken comes to receive his second dose of intravenous chemotherapy. Instead of the optimistic attitude and bright affect he had last week, Ken is withdrawn and has a flat affect. When asked how he is doing, he replies, "The past three weeks have been so hard. I had no idea how painful chemo would be and how persistent the nausea and vomiting have been. I have no strength. I have been praying, other people have been praying for me and I thought I was going to be healed. I know God can heal and do the impossible. I have two sons who still need a father. Why has God chosen not to heal me? I don't know how long I can do this…"

What data from the current concern is important & RELEVANT; therefore it has clinical significance to the nurse?

RELEVANT Data from Current Concern:	Clinical Significance:
Instead of the optimistic attitude and bright affect he had last week, Ken is withdrawn and has a flat affect.	*Pay attention to non-verbal communication! Remember that what is NOT spoken comprises the majority of what is communicated in any interaction. If appropriate, do not hesitate to ask a clarifying question to evaluate the patient's response and provide support as needed.*
When asked how he is doing he replies, "The past three weeks have been so hard. I had no idea how painful chemo would be and how persistent the nausea and vomiting have been. I have no strength.	*The physiologic effects of chemotherapy must never be underestimated by the nurse. Intravenous chemotherapy causes devastating side effects that many patients are unprepared for until they have experienced them: Severe nausea and vomiting, painful tingling with altered sensation, severe fatigue, and the loss of body hair and ulcers throughout the oral mucosa that make eating/drinking painful are common.*
I have been praying, other people have been praying for me and I thought I was going to be healed. I know God can heal and do the impossible. I have two sons who still need a father. Why has God chosen not to heal me? I don't know how long I can do this…	*This could be the beginning of a crisis of faith that could lead to spiritual distress.* *NANDA defines spiritual distress as "the disruption in the life principle that pervades a person's entire being and that integrates and transcends one's biological and psychosocial nature." A patient in spiritual distress loses hope, questions their belief system, or feels separated from personal sources of comfort and strength (Gulanick et al., 2003)* *The Bible is filled with numerous examples of God's ability and power to heal. The ministry of Jesus in the New Testament is comprised of numerous examples of miraculous healings, including Jesus raising the dead, healing the blind and lame. In addition, there are verses that support the power of faith to see God's power move if one believes.* *An important theological concept that can be derived from the scriptures is that God is also sovereign. Though God can heal, what if He chooses not to? This is an example of the sovereignty of God. Some are healed, but not all. This example is present even in the scriptures. But when you are the one who is NOT being healed and were expecting a different outcome, how should the nurse respond? It is important to understand some of the Biblical scriptures that Christians believe and how this relates to the beliefs that Christians hold especially in the context of illness.* *These scriptures include the following:* *Psalm 103:2-3 Praise the LORD,[1] O my soul, and forget not[2] all his benefits*

	who forgives all your sins[3] and heals[4] all your diseases .
	Mathew 9:35 And Jesus went throughout all the cities and villages, teaching in their synagogues and proclaiming the gospel of the kingdom and healing every disease and every affliction.
	Luke 1:37 For with God nothing will be impossible.
	James 5:13-16 Is anyone among you suffering? Let him pray. Is anyone cheerful? Let him sing praise. [14] Is anyone among you sick? Let him call for the elders of the church, and let them pray over him, anointing him with oil in the name of the Lord. [15] And the prayer of faith will save the one who is sick, and the Lord will raise him up. And if he has committed sins, he will be forgiven. [16] Therefore, confess your sins to one another and pray for one another, that you may be healed. The prayer of a righteous person has great power as it is working.

III. Resolving the Dilemma

1. Identifying data that is RELEVANT, what is the essence of this current dilemma?

Though there are physiologic needs as a result of his chemotherapy, such as Ken's current fatigue and pain, one filter that the nurse uses in practice to identify care priorities is also used on the NCLEX is to discriminate between the EXPECTED and the UNEXPECTED. Though the physiologic needs typically take priority and need to be addressed, these side effects are EXPECTED. What is UNEXPECTED are Ken's statements that indicate he is in some form of spiritual distress.

Recognizing this as an UNEXPECTED concern, the nurse must identify the essence of this current scenario as spiritual distress because Ken appears to have lost hope and is questioning his belief system as he wonders why God has not healed him.

2. What additional information is needed by the nurse that would help clarify the current dilemma?

What spiritual support does Ken have in the community and has he used this support recently? How has Ken been feeling physically most recently? Is he getting enough sleep? An individual becomes increasingly vulnerable to hopelessness and despair when one is physically exhausted or separated from sources of support. Though adequate rest and spiritual/psychosocial support will likely not completely alleviate the distress that Ken is experiencing, it can decrease the intensity and severity of these feelings.

To obtain additional information to clarify spiritual needs or assessment, here is some practical guidance that students will need:

How to practically assess spirituality at the end of life

This patient is at the end of life and spiritual issues often surface at this point, though they may not be readily apparent. Spiritual assessment for this patient might be explored with the FICA acronym. This model is useful for any faith belief system. FICA acronym represents:

- **F-Faith or beliefs:** *What are your spiritual beliefs? Do you consider yourself spiritual? What things do you believe in that give meaning to life?*
- **I-Importance and influence:** *Is faith important to you? How has your illness or hospitalization affected your personal belief practices?*
- **C-Community:** *Are you connected to a faith center in the community? Does it provide support/comfort for you during times of stress? Is there a person/group who assists you in your spirituality?*
- **A-Address:** *What can I do for you? What support can health care provide to support your spiritual beliefs/practices? (Dameron, 2005).*

These questions would naturally explore this patient's spirituality. It is always best if the nurse has some comfort with the exploration of spirituality. Patients can sense discomfort or anxiety in approaching this portion of the assessment. The FICA model offers some open ended questions to make spiritual assessment a natural part of the conversation. Use this spiritual assessment tool to make caring for the spirit an essential component of your nursing practice!

3. What additional members of the healthcare team could be used in this situation? Why?
A chaplain would be the most obvious and best outside resource that the nurse should attempt to use. He or she should also try to contact Ken's pastor or spiritual leader in the community. Obtain the patient's consent before initiating these interventions.

4. What is the nursing priority?
Spiritual distress.

Identifying the essence of the patient scenario and correctly determining the nursing priority is a foundational aspect of clinical reasoning. In any clinical scenario, the nursing priority may or may NOT be a NANDA nursing diagnosis. The following NANDA nursing diagnostic statements capture the essence of this scenario include:
- *Hopelessness*
- *Grieving*
- *Ineffective coping*

5. What nursing interventions and/or principles can the nurse use to successfully resolve this clinical dilemma?

Nursing care for a patient in spiritual distress involves the following foundational aspects:

1. *A caring, nurse-patient relationship. Patients report that their distress was relieved when the nurse cared for them holistically, provided freedom of choice when possible and when the nurse simply listened and gave the patient a chance to talk (Creel, 2007; Sellers, 2001).*
2. *Spirituality is a coping mechanism that can be used by patients to transcend their current illness and suffering and provide meaning (Emblem & Halstead, 1993).*
3. *Active listening and facilitating the patient's verbalization of concerns are foundational to spiritual care.*
4. *Nurses do not need to know about specific beliefs, religions or spiritual practices to provide effective spiritual care (Martin, Burrows and Pomillo, 1983).*
5. *Spiritual care involves communicating respect for the patient, listening and appropriate self-disclosure (Sellers, 2001; Taylor, 2003).*

The essence of spiritual care is providing hope when life appears hopeless. There are numerous caring interventions that the nurse can use to actively demonstrate support and care for this patient in a time of crisis. These interventions comprise the essence of the "art" of nursing and could include the following:

- *Respect and support the patient's faith and religious belief system by making appropriate referrals.*
- *Acknowledge the patient's suffering and act to ease suffering by showing compassion.*
- *Allow the patient to verbalize anger and fear.*
- *Help the patient deal with feelings of guilt and instill hope (Villagomeza, 2005).*

Additional principles that are foundational to spiritual care include the following:
Nurse presence.
*When the nurse is present and with the patient in a non-hurried manner, this clearly communicates caring and support that Ken needs at this time. Presence for the nurse is being present in the moment with the patient and **his** moment, which is happening **now**. The emotional breakthroughs don't last long, but it's critical for nurses to connect with the patient. Patients sense whether the nurse is willing to "go there" or not. If they sense you are not willing to be in the moment with them, they will pull back and the moment ends. If the nurse fiddles with the computer or indicates nonverbally a discomfort with what is happening, it will decrease trust with the nurse.*

Patients don't care how much you know until they know how much you care. This is about focusing on the patient and caring responses to build trust. It truly is a privilege for the nurse to have a patient share the "tough stuff" in life with you. Generally, the patient will not share like this unless they trust you or they are in an affective domain crisis. This patient is in crisis of belief and ready for a breakthrough moment. The question is, will the nurse be willing to go there with him?

Silence. It is important to recognize that there are situations where no words are needed. Sitting in silence with a patient does not need to be awkward but indirectly communicates presence as well as caring which will support the patient in this crisis. Pauses can be productive for patients to process what is happening to them. After the silence, be willing to listen and go where the patient takes you.

Touch.
Reaching out and touching the patient's hand or shoulder and assessing the response to this intervention would also communicate caring and support.

Open-ended spiritual assessment questions.
There are a number of questions that the nurse can select from to ask a patient in spiritual crisis. At times asking one question will open up the conversation and the patient will begin to share openly.
   o *What is your source of strength, peace, faith, hope, and worth?*
   o *What spiritual practices are important to you?*
   o *What can I do to support your faith?*

Prayer.
Just as there are sometimes moments where there is nothing to say, there are times where it is equally apparent that the most effective and appropriate nursing intervention is to pray. It is essential that the nurse also recognizes the value of faith and spirituality in his/her own life and has something to offer and give.

My faith is an essential component of who I am. I am comfortable addressing matters of the spirit when they arise in caring for others. Do not underestimate the power of prayer and the comfort it can provide to patients. I have yet to have a patient decline an offer for prayer when I sensed it was appropriate to go there.

A response I frequently use is, "God is waiting for you. He cares about you."

The follow-up could be "Would you like me to pray with you? How would you like me to pray?"

Only if the nurse is comfortable with prayer, pray with the patient. JACHO recognizes that it is ok for nurses to pray with patients as long as they have permission from the patient and are attentive to pray in a way that is meaningful to the patient.
Support and encourage students whose faith and spirituality is important to them by reminding them that he/she can pray for their patients privately as they provide care. This will also facilitate needed nurse engagement.

Pitfalls to avoid in addressing issues of spiritual distress include:

* *Trying to solve the patient's problems or resolve unanswerable questions.*
* *Going beyond the nurse's role or expertise or imposing personal spiritual beliefs on the patient.*
* *Providing premature reassurance to the patient (Lo, B. et al., 2002).*

6. What is the expected patient response that indicates nursing interventions were effective?
The essence of spiritual care is providing hope. If the patient communicates a sense of hope or even verbalizes his feelings, it would be considered a step in the right direction. Pay close attention to non-verbal communication that would indicate engagement and hope, such as eye contact and a brighter affect.

7. What patient response would indicate that a change in the plan of care and nursing interventions are needed?
If Ken's non-verbal communication continues to demonstrate a flat, depressed affect and there is a lack of eye contact as well as ongoing expressions of hopelessness, these would all be signs that further intervention and support are needed.

8. What is the patient or family likely experiencing/feeling right now in this situation?
Though Ken's experience has been clearly delineated in this scenario, the needs of the wife and children must also be considered by the nurse. This patient is relatively young, with a wife and two teenage children. This creates obvious feelings of anxiety for them, and grief over the possible loss of a husband and father. Though the patient is clearly in spiritual crisis, it is also important to determine if the wife is struggling in similar ways and also requires spiritual support. Remember the importance of caring not only for the needs of the patient but also for the family. This is the essence of holistic care!

9. What can I do to engage myself with this patient's experience, and show that he matters to me as a person?
The essence of empathy is to put oneself in the shoes of those you are caring for or the family and how they are responding. If the nurse can consciously make this transition, it becomes much easier to be moved with a heart of compassion for those that one cares for.

Swanson (1991) identified the following caring interventions in the practice setting that have relevance in this scenario to engage with this patient's experience and support both the patient and family in this crisis:

Family caring interventions
- Maintain a hope-filled attitude
- Offer realistic optimism
- Support the family
- Explain all that is taking place and answer any/all questions
- Convey availability to the family

Patient caring interventions
- Preserve the dignity of the patient
- Anticipate needs
- Comfort the patient in any way
- Seek cues by paying close attention to the patient's response and anticipate her expected response
- Perform competently and skillfully as a nurse. This communicates caring to your patient!
- Convey availability to the patient

10. What was learned from this case study that you will incorporate into your practice?
Content knowledge without personal application will not be fruitful. Reflection is an essential professional behavior that can also be practiced! I have added this question to allow students to intentionally reflect on what they have learned so that they can integrate this essential content into their practice and fully develop the ethical comportment of the professional nurse. This question will facilitate rich dialogue in whatever context you choose to use this case study. If there is not enough time to discuss this question, consider having students write a one-page reflection paper.

References

Creel, E. (2007). The meaning of spiritual nursing acre for ill individuals with no religious affiliation. *International Journal for Human Caring* 11(3): 14-21.

Dameron, C.M. (2005). Spiritual assessment made easy…With acronyms! *Journal of Christian Nursing*, 22, 14-16.

Emblem, J. D. & Halstead, L. (1993). Spiritual needs and interventions: Comparing the views of patients, nurses and chaplains. *Clinical Nurse Specialist* 7(4): 175-182.

Gulanick, M. , Myers, J., Klopp, A., et al. (2003) *Nursing Care Plans: Nursing Diagnosis and Intervention.* 5th ed. St. Louis: Mosby

Lo, B., Ruston, D., Kates, L.W. et al. (2002). Discussing religious and spiritual issues at the end of life: A practical guide for physicians. *Journal of the American Medical Association.* 287(6): 749-754.

Martin, C., Burrows, C., & Pomilio, J. (1983). Spiritual needs of patients study. In Fish, S. & Shelly J. (Eds) *Spiritual care: The nurse's role.* Downer's Grove, IL: Intervarsity Press.

Sellers, S. (2001). The spiritual care meanings of adults residing in the Midwest. *Nursing Science Quarterly* 14 (3): 239-249.

Swanson, K. M. (1991). Empirical development of a middle range theory of caring. *Nursing Research, 40*(3), 161–166.

Taylor, E.J. (2007) *What Do I Say? Talking with Patients about Spirituality.* Templeton Press: Philadelphia.

Villagomeza, L. R. (2005). Spiritual distress in adult cancer patients. *Holistic Nursing Practice.* November/December: 285-294.

TREATMENT Dilemma

Surgery or Medical Management

STUDENT Worksheet

Mohammed Abdi, 82 years old

Overview

When a patient requires surgery to save his life, most will choose this option with no reservations. But what if surgery requires lengthy rehabilitation and a colostomy for the rest of his life? Medical management is an option, but has less than a 50-50 chance of surviving. How can the nurse can ensure that the patient fully understands all treatment options when there is both a language and a cultural barrier is the essence of this dilemma.

Surgery or Medical Management

I. Scenario

History of Present Problem:

Mohammed Abdi is an 82-year-old who was admitted to the ED for severe abdominal pain with right sided tenderness the past six hours. An abdominal CT scan confirmed that he has acute diverticulitis with moderate amount of intraperitoneal free air throughout the abdomen. His WBC is 19.8 with neutrophils of 95%. He has a current temp of 101.2 (oral), heart rate of 98, respiratory rate of 18, and blood pressure of 102/58.

The general surgeon has been consulted and communicates to Mohammed that he will need immediate surgery to wash out the abdomen and remove bowel contents that have spilled into the peritoneum. The surgery will also require the need for a permanent colostomy and 2-4 weeks of acute and transitional care. Mohammed is clearly apprehensive about having a "bag of poop" attached to his body the rest of his life and wants to know if there are any other options.

Personal/Social History:

Mohammed is Muslim and emigrated from Somalia ten years ago. He understands little English. He lives alone in an assisted living apartment. His wife died ten years ago. He has one daughter who lives in the local area and is active in his life.

What data from the histories is important & RELEVANT; therefore it has clinical significance to the nurse?

RELEVANT Data from Present Problem:	Clinical Significance:
RELEVANT Data from Social History:	Clinical Significance:

II. The Dilemma Begins…

Current Concern:

The surgeon proposes another alternative that would involve more conservative medical management. Instead of having surgery and a colostomy, Mohammed's bowel perforation could be treated with IV antibiotics and his response monitor closely. In some cases, the body is able to seal the bowel perforation spontaneously if it is small enough. The likelihood of this outcome is less than 50%. If medical management is not successful, he is at an extremely high risk of sepsis progressing to septic shock that would make him unsuitable to be surgically treated and he would likely die as a result. He comments to the nurse through an interpreter after the surgeon has left, "I have lived a good life and have pleased Allah. I am ready to go to paradise."

What data from the current concern is important & RELEVANT; therefore it has clinical significance to the nurse?

RELEVANT Data from Current Concern:	Clinical Significance:

III. Resolving the Dilemma

1. Identifying data that is RELEVANT, what is the essence of this current dilemma?

2. What additional information is needed by the nurse that would help clarify the current dilemma?

3. What additional members of the healthcare team could be used in this situation? Why?

4. What is the nursing priority?

5. What nursing interventions and/or principles can the nurse use to successfully resolve this clinical dilemma?

6. What is the expected response of the patient that indicate the nursing interventions were effective?

7. What response by the patient would indicate that a change in the plan of care and nursing interventions are needed?

8. What is the patient and family likely experiencing/feeling right now in this situation?

9. What can I do to engage myself with this patient's experience, and show that he matters to me as a person?

10. What was learned from this case study that you will incorporate into your practice?

TREATMENT Dilemma
Surgery or Medical Management

Mohammed Abdi, 82 years old

Answer Key

Clinical Dilemma Activity: ANSWER KEY
Surgery or Medical Management
I. Scenario
History of Present Problem:

Mohammed Abdi is an 82-year-old who was admitted to the ED for severe abdominal pain with right sided tenderness the past six hours. An abdominal CT scan confirmed that he has acute diverticulitis with moderate amount of intraperitoneal free air throughout the abdomen. His WBC is 19.8 with neutrophils of 95%. He has a current temp of 101.2 (oral), heart rate of 98, respiratory rate of 18, and blood pressure of 102/58.

The general surgeon has been consulted and communicates to Mohammed that he will need immediate surgery to wash out the abdomen and remove bowel contents that have spilled into the peritoneum. The surgery will also require the need for a permanent colostomy and 2-4 weeks of acute and transitional care. Mohammed is clearly apprehensive about having a "bag of poop" attached to his body the rest of his life and wants to know if there are any other options.

Personal/Social History:

Mohammed is Muslim and emigrated from Somalia ten years ago. He understands little English. He lives alone in an assisted living apartment. His wife died ten years ago. He has one daughter who lives in the local area and is active in his life.

What data from the histories is important & RELEVANT; therefore it has clinical significance to the nurse?

RELEVANT Data from Present Problem:	Clinical Significance:
82-year-old male who was admitted to the ED for severe abdominal pain with right sided tenderness the past six hours.	*The age of this patient must be noted by the nurse. Mohammed is an elder elderly at the age of 82. Regardless of the physiologic problem, a patient of this age is more likely to be more fragile and at a higher risk for complications. Of the five rights of clinical reasoning (1), the "right patient" who is at higher risk of complications must be recognized by the nurse and must have a higher level of vigilance for the potential development of complications.*
An abdominal CT scan confirmed that he has acute diverticulitis with moderate amount of intraperitoneal free air throughout the abdomen.	*The relationship between severe abdominal pain, acute diverticulitis, and intraperitoneal free air in the abdomen must be recognized as a significant clinical RED FLAG! The free air confirms the problem of a likely ruptured diverticulum that has caused leakage of air and with it bowel contents into the sterile peritoneum of the abdomen. This is an obvious problem and urgent action is required!*
His WBC is 19.8 with neutrophils of 95%. He has a current temp of 101.2 (oral), heart rate of 98, respiratory rate of 18, and blood pressure of 102/58.	*This cluster of clinical data must be recognized as a systemic inflammatory response likely related to early sepsis. This clinical data is relevant and must be carefully trended by the nurse. Trending the most important clinical data is a foundational aspect of clinical reasoning.*
He will need immediate surgery to wash out the abdomen and remove bowel contents that have spilled into the peritoneum.	*The surgeon has confirmed that immediate surgery is needed to best resolve this problem.*
The surgery will also require the need for a permanent colostomy and 2-4 weeks of acute and transitional care.	*Unfortunately, the surgery will require a colostomy and extensive time for rehabilitation. For a patient of this age, the recovery will be longer and not tolerated as well if this surgery was performed when he was younger.*
Mohammed is clearly apprehensive about having a "bag of poop" attached to his body the rest of his life and wants to know if there are any other options.	*Mohammed is mentally alert and clearly understands the implications of surgery. Having a colostomy is a significant disfigurement of body image. Therefore, it is understandable that he would want to know if there are any other options to resolve his current problem.*

RELEVANT Data from Social History:	Clinical Significance:
Mohammed is Muslim and emigrated from Somalia ten years ago. He understands little English.	*The faith tradition and country of origin of the patient is relevant and must be noted. If large immigrant groups are present in the community where the nurse works, it is imperative to become culturally competent and provide culturally sensitive care. The language barrier is also relevant and appropriate interpretation services will be needed. Though family, if present, may interpret in a crisis, when there is a need to communicate the plan of care with life and death consequences, a translator MUST be present.*
Mohammed lives alone in an assisted living apartment.	*Though living alone is not uncommon for the elderly, it must be noted that Mohammed is 82 years old. To be live alone in this context demonstrates that he is a high functioning elder elderly and is used to a high level of autonomy and independence at this stage in his life.*
His wife died ten years ago. He has one daughter who is local and active in his life.	*It is important for the nurse to identify social support available to an elderly patient. His wife's death has not been recent and he has likely worked through his grief. But he does have a daughter who is involved and active in his life and can provide support as needed regardless of the choice that Mohammed makes regarding surgery.*

II. The Dilemma Begins…

Current Concern:

The surgeon proposes another alternative that would involve more conservative medical management. Instead of having surgery and a colostomy, Mohammed's bowel perforation could be treated with IV antibiotics and his response monitor closely. In some cases, the body is able to seal the bowel perforation spontaneously if it is small enough. The likelihood of this outcome is less than 50%. If medical management is not successful, he is at an extremely high risk of sepsis progressing to septic shock that would make him unsuitable to be surgically treated and he would likely die as a result. He comments to the nurse through an interpreter after the surgeon has left, "I have lived a good life and have pleased Allah. I am ready to go to paradise."

What data from the current concern is important & RELEVANT; therefore it has clinical significance to the nurse?

RELEVANT Data from Current Concern:	Clinical Significance:
His bowel perforation could be treated with IV antibiotics and closely monitor his response. In some cases the body is able to seal the bowel perforation spontaneously if it is small enough.	*This information from the surgeon makes it clear that Mohammed does have a viable alternative if he does not want to undergo the stress and pain, of surgery and the resultant colostomy bag for the rest of his life.*
The likelihood of this outcome is less than 50%.	*Though surgery is not without risk, his odds would be better to undergo the surgery. To not have the surgery is pretty much a coin flip and could easily go either way.*
If medical management is not successful, he is at an extremely high risk of sepsis progressing to septic shock that would make him unsuitable to be surgically treated and he would likely die as a result.	*It is important for the nurse to note that the most likely complication that Mohammed would experience if he did not respond to IV antibiotics is septic shock. Mohammed has already demonstrated early signs of sepsis with an elevated white blood cell count and neutrophil percentage, as well as vital signs that represent an elevation of heart rate and a blood pressure that is currently soft. All of this clinical data must be carefully trended by the nurse if Mohammed chooses not to undergo surgery to determine the trajectory of his status and response to conservative medical treatment. This is the essence of clinical reasoning.* *If Mohammed did respond well to IV antibiotics, the nurse would expect to see his white blood cell count and neutrophil percentage decrease*

	over the next 24 to 48 hours. His temperature and heart rate would also decrease. His blood pressure trend would increase over time compared to his current.
He comments to the nurse through an interpreter after the surgeon has left, "I have lived a good life and have pleased Allah. I am ready to go to paradise."	This statement is significant and demonstrates why this patient is more comfortable with a conservative approach to managing his present problem. The power of an authentic faith in a patient can strongly influence how current problems are viewed and filtered when this lens of faith is present. Though the nurse may not be Muslim, it is important for the nurse to support, understand the patient's faith traditions and seek common ground.

III. Resolving the Dilemma

1. Identifying data that is RELEVANT, what is the essence of this current dilemma?
The essence of this scenario is the decision to pursue aggressive and needed surgical management to resolve the bowel perforation or to conservatively manage his case without surgery, knowing that it is more likely that Mohammed will die as a result. This scenario illustrates the importance of the ethical concept of autonomy and the right of a competent patient to make their own choice knowing the implications of each alternative.

2. What additional information is needed by the nurse that would help clarify the current dilemma?
Because this patient is clearly competent and has no cognitive impairments, there is no significant additional information needed to clarify this dilemma. The patient has the right to make this difficult choice. Because Mohammed has expressed aspects related to his faith that likely influence his decision to consider a more conservative course, it would be appropriate for the nurse to explore this further to obtain clarification as needed. The following open-ended spiritual assessment questions include the:
- Are you connected with a faith community?
- What is your source of strength, peace, faith, hope, and worth?
- What spiritual practices are important to you?
- What can I do to support your faith?
- What makes life meaningful for you?
- What do you feel is the meaning of all that you are currently experiencing?

By building on the patient's responses and asking any one of these open-ended spiritual assessment questions, the nurse can use this information to provide spiritual care and support. It would also be appropriate to ask the patient's permission to obtain a chaplain referral.

3. What additional members of the healthcare team could be used in this situation? Why?
If Mohammed consents to a chaplain visit, this would be an additional source of support regarding his decision to pursue a conservative management that may result in death. The nurse could also offer to contact his imam or spiritual leader in the community who could provide more personal spiritual care and support.

4. What is the nursing priority?
There is no clear NANDA nursing diagnostic statement that fits well with this scenario. It is enough for the nurse to simply make it a priority to support and ensure that there are no knowledge deficits related to the choices that he must make regarding surgery or conservative management.

5. What nursing interventions and/or principles can the nurse use to successfully resolve this clinical dilemma?
It is important that the nurse maintains a caring, supportive, and nonjudgmental attitude about Mohammed's choice. If the nurse feels strongly that he should have surgery, for example, it is important to NOT communicate this verbally as well as nonverbally to the patient. It is important for the nurse to have a high level of awareness of the message his or her body language conveys.

The nurse can expect changes in this patient's condition as he could be unstable. Appropriate interventions for the *physical domain might include the following: frequent assessment of the trend in vital signs, and hydration as a fluid shift can be anticipated due to bowel problem and patient is NPO. Attention to comfort measures such as positioning and perhaps a back rub are a priority in the "watch and wait" period of time. Secondly, the nurse needs to be attentive to the affective domain.*

Expect the patient to want and have the need to share what he is feeling and experiencing in this moment. Be willing to ask open-ended questions that would allow this expression of feelings. Anything that the nurse can do to demonstrate care and concern will be appreciated as well by the patient in this context. Other caring nursing interventions that would be appropriate include:

- ***Nurse presence.*** *When the nurse is present and with the patient in a non-hurried manner, this clearly communicates caring and support that Mohammed needs at this time. Listening carefully to the patient to determineg the overall "message" of what is being communicated is an essential nursing intervention. Use the therapeutic communication skill of paraphrasing to communicate clearly to the patient that they have been "heard" by the nurse.*

- ***Silence.*** *It is important to recognize that there are situations where no words are needed. Sitting in silence with a patient in this context does not need to be awkward but indirectly communicates presence as well as caring which will support the patient.*

- ***Touch.*** *Reaching out and touching the patient's hand or shoulder and assessing the response to this intervention would also communicate caring and support in this scenario. One cannot know how a patient will receive touch so the nurse must first assess the patient response. If the nurse allows the patient in control to withdraw touch, it simplifies evaluation of the intervention of touch. One simple way to implement this approach is to slip your hand under the patient's hand with your palm up. The patient can withdraw their hand at any time if the nurse's hand is not on top of the patient's hand and provides needed control for the patient.*

- ***Prayer.*** *The spiritual domain also needs to be acknowledged with this patient. The nurse might ask, "Would you like me to pray with you?" If the answer is yes, ask the patient, "What do you want me to pray for?" Only if the nurse is comfortable with prayer, pray with the patient. JACHO recognizes that it is ok for nurses to pray with patients as long as they have permission from the patient and are attentive to pray in a way meaningful to the patient.*

*Just as there are sometimes moments when silence and remaining present are appropriate, there are times when it is equally apparent that the most effective and appropriate nursing intervention is to pray. It it is essential that the nurse also recognizes the value of faith and spirituality in his/her own life and has something to offer and give. **Support and encourage students whose faith and spirituality is important to them by reminding them that he/she can pray for their patients privately as they provide care. This will also facilitate needed nurse engagement.***

My faith is an essential component of who I am. I am comfortable addressing matters of the spirit when they arise n caring for others. Do not underestimate the power of prayer and the comfort it can provide to patients. I have yet to have a patient decline an offer for prayer when I sensed it was appropriate to do so. This can still be done even if the patient's faith tradition is different than the nurse's, but must be done with sensitivity.

6. What is the expected response of the patient that indicate the nursing interventions were effective?
The nurse would expect the patient to remain calm and peaceful despite the storm that he faces. Comfort measures are also indicated that would include the treatment of pain and the prompt implementation of IV antibiotics if the patient chooses conservative medical management.

7. What response from the patient would indicate that a change in the plan of care and nursing interventions are needed?
If the patient expressed doubt or changed his mind regarding what he feels is best or even asks the nurse what he or she would do, this indicates that he is not convinced that this is the best decision to make. If Mohammed were to demonstrate any of these behaviors, it would be important for the nurse to contact the surgeon and to clarify the patient's questions.

8. What is the patient and family likely experiencing/feeling right now in this situation?

The patient does not appear to be in any distress over the decision to pursue a more conservative medical management. What is not known is how the daughter feels about this decision. It is not uncommon for the family to want everything done and not be at peace with a decision that does not include doing everything that is possible to "fix" the current medical problem.

9. What can I do to engage myself with this patient's experience, and show that he matters to me as a person?

The essence of empathy is to put oneself in the shoes of those you are caring for or the family and how they are responding. If the nurse can consciously make this transition, it becomes much easier to be moved with a heart of compassion for those that one cares for.

Swanson (1991) the following caring interventions in the practice setting that have relevance in this scenario to engage in this patient's experience and support both the patient and family in this crisis:

Family caring interventions
- *Maintain a hope-filled attitude*
- *Offer realistic optimism*
- *Support the family*
- *Explain all that is taking place and answer any/all questions*
- *Convey availability to the family*

Patient caring interventions
- *Preserve the dignity of the patient*
- *Anticipate needs*
- *Comfort the patient in any way*
- *Seek cues by paying close attention to the patient's response and anticipate her expected response*
- *Perform competently and skillfully as a nurse. This communicates caring to your patient!*
- *Convey availability to the patient*

10. What was learned from this case study that you will incorporate into your practice?

Content knowledge without personal application will not be fruitful. Reflection is an essential professional behavior that can also be practiced! I have added this question to allow students to intentionally reflect on what they have learned so that they can integrate this essential content into their practice and fully develop the ethical comportment of the professional nurse. This question will facilitate rich dialogue in whatever context you choose to use this case study. If there is not enough time to discuss this question, consider having students write a one-page reflection paper.

References:

Levett-Jones, T., Hoffman, K., Dempsey, J., Yeun-Sim Jeong, S., Noble, D., Norton, C. Hickey, N. (2010). The 'five rights' of clinical reasoning: An educational model to enhance nursing students' ability to identify and manage clinically 'at risk' patients. Nurse Education Today, 30, 515–520.

Swanson, K. M. (1991). Empirical development of a middle range theory of caring. *Nursing Research, 40*(3), 161–166.

TREATMENT Dilemma

Dialysis or Hospice

STUDENT Worksheet

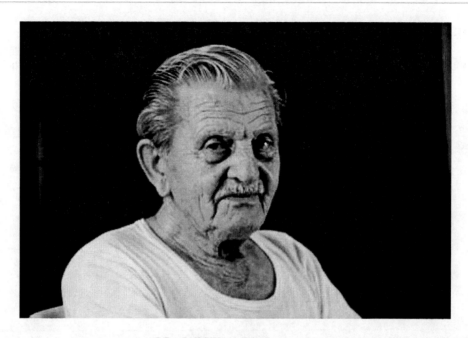

Mark Miller, 82 years old

Overview

Though aggressive medical management is expected with a critically ill patient, there comes a time when the paths of quality of life and quantity of life intersect and the patient must make a choice. How the nurse can practically care and support a patient with end stage heart failure who needs to choose between dialysis for the rest of his life or hospice is the essence of this dilemma.

Clinical Dilemma Activity: STUDENT

Dialysis or Hospice

I. Scenario

History of Present Problem:

Mark Miller is an 82-year-old man who was admitted to the hospital eight days ago with heart failure exacerbation. He has a history of coronary artery disease, myocardial infarction, atrial fibrillation, ischemic cardiomyopathy with a current ejection fraction of 15%, bi-ventricular pacemaker/ICD and chronic renal failure (stage III) that will soon require dialysis. He is unable to tolerate minimal activity without becoming SOB. His creatinine is 2.7 and despite diuresis with furosemide IV continuous drip, his urine output has been averaging 600 mL the last two days. His current weight is up 8 kilograms from his last hospitalization three weeks ago.

Personal/Social History:

Mark has been married to his wife Susan for sixty years who remains the love of his life. He considers himself a driven type A personality who has become increasingly frustrated with his current limitations to activity. They have three children who are involved and live in the community. He currently lives in his own home and is independent, though his wife assists with meals and laundry.

What data from the histories is important & RELEVANT; therefore it has clinical significance to the nurse?

RELEVANT Data from Present Problem:	Clinical Significance:
RELEVANT Data from Social History:	**Clinical Significance:**

II. The Dilemma Begins...

Current Concern:

As Mark examines his current prognosis, he recognizes that undergoing dialysis for the rest of his life is not something he is sure he wants to pursue. He has lived a fulfilling life as a husband, father, grandfather, and retired attorney. His wife wants him to do everything possible that will keep them together as a couple.

What data from the current concern is important & RELEVANT; therefore it has clinical significance to the nurse?

RELEVANT Data from Current Concern:	Clinical Significance:

III. Resolving the Dilemma

1. Identifying data that is RELEVANT, what is the essence of this current dilemma?

2. What additional information is needed by the nurse that would help clarify the current dilemma?

3. What additional members of the healthcare team could be used in this situation? Why?

4. What is the nursing priority?

5. What nursing interventions and/or principles can the nurse use to successfully resolve this clinical dilemma?

6. What is the expected response of the patient that indicate the nursing interventions were effective?

7. What response by the patient would indicate that a change in the plan of care and nursing interventions are needed?

8. What is the patient likely experiencing/feeling right now in this situation?

9. What can I do to engage myself with this patient's experience, and show that he matters to me as a person?

10. What was learned from this case study that you will incorporate into your practice?

TREATMENT Dilemma

Dialysis or Hospice

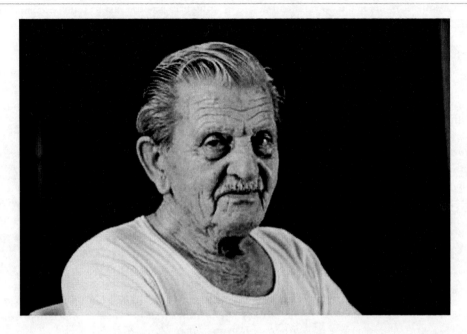

Mark Miller, 82 years old

Answer Key

Dialysis or Hospice

I. Scenario

History of Present Problem:

Mark Miller is an 82-year-old man who was admitted to the hospital eight days ago with heart failure exacerbation. He has a history of coronary artery disease, myocardial infarction, atrial fibrillation, ischemic cardiomyopathy with a current ejection fraction of 15%, bi-ventricular pacemaker/ICD and chronic renal failure (stage III) that will soon require dialysis. He is unable to tolerate minimal activity without becoming SOB. His creatinine is 2.7 and despite diuresis with furosemide IV continuous drip, his urine output has been averaging 600 mL the last two days. His current weight is up 8 kilograms from his last hospitalization three weeks ago.

Personal/Social History:

Mark has been married to his wife Susan for sixty years, She remains the love of his life. He considers himself a driven type A personality who has become increasingly frustrated with his current limitations to activity. They have three children who are involved and reside in the community. He currently lives in his own home and is independent, though his wife assists with meals and laundry.

What data from the histories is important & RELEVANT; therefore it has clinical significance to the nurse?

RELEVANT Data from Present Problem:	**Clinical Significance:**
82-year-old man who was admitted to the hospital eight days ago with heart failure exacerbation.	*The age of the patient is always relevant. Though he is 82 and elderly, the average life expectancy of men in the US is 76, so he is above average. The older the patient, the more likely he or she will experience higher rates of complications with any procedures or the reason they are hospitalized.*
	Of the five rights of clinical reasoning, the "right" patient must always be considered as one who may be at higher risk for an adverse outcome because of age or other factors such as altered immune status or chronic illnesses (Levett–Jones et al., 2010).
He has a history of coronary artery disease, myocardial infarction, atrial fibrillation, ischemic cardiomyopathy with a current ejection fraction of 15%, bi-ventricular pacemaker/ICD and chronic renal failure (stage III) that will soon require dialysis.	*An important component of thinking like a nurse is the ability to identify relationships of clinical data. In the context of Mark's medical problems, it is important for the nurse to recognize that this cluster of medical problems did not develop in isolation. Each one of these illnesses are related to the others. They are like dominoes that begin to fall. When one starts, the other problems develop as a result. His coronary artery disease led to the myocardial infarction which was likely responsible for causing the development of the ischemic cardiomyopathy that led to end-stage heart failure with an ejection fraction (EF) of only 15%. As a result of the poor perfusion to the kidneys, Mark has developed stage III kidney disease. This is not uncommon with many patients who have heart failure.*
	Another series of clinical relationships that students need to recognize is atrial fibrillation, heart failure, and the need for a biventricular pacemaker. Review the importance of atrial kick and how this is lost in atrial fibrillation. Atrial kick is a synchronized contraction of the atrium that contributes 25 to 30% of additional stroke volume. The loss of atrial kick has an obvious detrimental effect to cardiac output in a patient with heart failure. The biventricular pacemaker provides an electrical impulse to unify a contraction in the atrium as well as the ventricles, therefore improving cardiac output.

	15% ejection fraction is END STAGE heart failure and approaching incompatibility with life. Review normal EF (60-65%) and how low this is from a normal heart. Have students explain in their own words what ejection fraction is to ensure that they truly understand this concept and content.
He is unable to tolerate minimal activity without becoming SOB.	The inability to tolerate minimal activity without becoming short of breath is a clinical RED FLAG and indicates the severity of underlying heart failure.
His creatinine is 2.7 and despite diuresis with furosemide IV continuous drip, his urine output has been averaging 600 mL the last two days.	This cluster of data is extremely concerning when a deep understanding of heart failure, renal function, and furosemide is integrated together. When a normal creatinine is compared to this level of 2.7 it is clear that this is extremely elevated. Though he is averaging close to 30 mL of urine output volume, which is a textbook norm, when a furosemide drip -- the most powerful diuretic that can be administered -- barely produces the bare minimum of textbook norms, this is a clinical RED FLAG that must be recognized by the nurse. It is not enough!
His current weight is up 8 kilograms from his last hospitalization three weeks ago.	This piece of clinical data confirms that Mark's urine output is not enough! Remember that s weight increase of 8 kg means an additional 8000 mL of volume in the body. The additional workload of circulating this increased volume will easily cause significant and severe exacerbation of heart failure. The combination of this high amount of circulating fluid volume and the lack of an adequate response to a powerful loop diuretic is ominous. There is little that can be done to excrete the additional volume without dialysis, either short-term or likely long-term in this context.
RELEVANT Data from Social History:	**Clinical Significance:**
Mark has been married to his wife Susan for sixty years. She is the love of his life.	Never underestimate the power of a positive relationship and marriage to motivate a strong desire to live. This support is essential especially when discharge planning is being considered.
He considers himself a driven type A personality who has become increasingly frustrated with his current limitations to activity.	His frustration is clearly understandable. A driven type A values the need to have something to be done or to working on it. To lose this ability to be productive strikes at the core of one's being and the essence of who you are.
They have three children who are involved and reside in the community. He currently lives in his own home and is independent.	The importance of social and family support is essential for any patient and especially so for Mark. It is important to note that despite his chronic illness and end-stage heart failure he is able to maintain independence and live in his own home. Anything that would alter this reality will be devastating and its implications to his psychosocial well-being need to be considered.

II. The Dilemma Begins...

Current Concern:

As Mark examines his current prognosis, he recognizes that undergoing dialysis for the rest of his life is not something he is sure he wants to pursue. He has lived a fulfilling life as a husband, father, grandfather, and retired attorney. His wife wants him to do everything possible that will keep them together as a couple.

What data from the current concern is important & RELEVANT; therefore it has clinical significance to the nurse?

RELEVANT Data from Current Concern:	Clinical Significance:
Undergoing dialysis for the rest of his life is not something he is sure he wants to pursue.	*Because Mark is a competent adult and ironically a retired attorney, his right to autonomy and make a decision regarding undergoing dialysis or not must be supported.*
He has lived a fulfilling life as a husband, father, grandfather, and retired attorney. His wife wants him to do everything possible that will keep them together as a couple.	*Using Erickson's theory of psychosocial development, Mark is in the final stage of ego integrity versus despair. Mark clearly has no red flags for despair and can look back at his life with a sense of purpose and accomplishment and a life well lived. Though the wife's desire to keep Mark alive is understandable, **the patient's** desires and wishes are what really matters.*

III. Resolving the Dilemma

1. Identifying data that is RELEVANT, what is the essence of this current dilemma?
Mark has reached the terminal or end-stage phase of his heart failure. He needs to choose between medical management only which would lead to death in a short period of time, or be willing to consider dialysis and its likely long-term implications that will affect life as he has currently known it.

2. What additional information is needed by the nurse that would help clarify the current dilemma?
Though there is no hint of despair or spiritual distress, because Mark's condition represents a terminal state, and spiritual issues may arise as a result, it would be relevant to know if he has a faith tradition that is meaningful to him and how this can be supported if present.

How to practically assess spirituality
This patient is at the end of life and spiritual issues often surface at this point in life though they may not be readily apparent. Spiritual assessment for this patient might be explored with the FICA acronym. This model is useful for any faith belief system. FICA acronym represents:

- *F-Faith or beliefs: What are your spiritual beliefs? Do you consider yourself spiritual? What things do you believe in that give meaning to life?*
- *I-Importance and influence: Is faith important to you? How has your illness or hospitalization affected your personal belief practices?*
- *C-Community: Are you connected to a faith center in the community? Does it provide support/comfort for you during times of stress? Is there a person/group who assists you in your spirituality?*
- *A-Address: What can I do for you? What support can health care provide to support your spiritual beliefs/practices? (Dameron, 2005).*

These questions, if used by the nurse in this scenario, would naturally explore this patient's spirituality. It is always best if the nurse has some comfort with the exploration of spirituality. Patients can sense discomfort or anxiety in approaching this portion of the assessment. The FICA model offers some open-ended questions to make spiritual assessment a natural part of the conversation. Use this spiritual assessment tool to make caring for the spirit an essential component of your nursing practice!

3. What additional members of the healthcare team could be used in this situation? Why?
If Mark does have a faith tradition and would want a chaplain consult this would be appropriate. It would also be important to contact his pastor or spiritual leader in the community to provide a more personal level of involvement and support.
Social services may also be relevant if Mark chooses a more conservative approach and does not want to have dialysis but be discharged to home with hospice. This level of discharge planning needs the involvement of social services.

4. What is the nursing priority?
Knowledge deficit.

Though Mark is intelligent and is a retired attorney, the most important nursing priority is to ensure that he has full and thorough understanding of the treatment options of current medical management versus dialysis.

Include the FAMILY as much as possible in education. The spouse or significant other will be needed to reinforce what you are teaching once the patient is home.

Though the primary priority for the nurse is the patient, the nurse also cares for the family. Therefore, the needs of the wife must also be considered in this scenario. She will be directly affected by her husband's decision to forgo dialysis and his impending death. In order to care for the spouse in this scenario the nurse must consider the nursing priorities of:
- *knowledge deficit*
- *risk for loneliness*
- *anxiety*
- *powerlessness*

Another approach to setting nursing priorities is to consider the patient/families priorities. Here is a simple question to get to the essence of family care priorities: If you only had ONE question to ask and then go home today, what would you want answered today? This identifies the most pressing issue or concern. It is helpful to consider the patient and nursing priorities when determining where your teaching efforts should be focused. This builds trust because the patient/families know you genuinely care about them (Wright & Leahey, 1999).

5. What nursing interventions and/or principles can the nurse use to successfully resolve this clinical dilemma?
Though the nurse practitioner or specialty educator will be responsible for primary education, it is important that the primary nurse has a strong working knowledge of all aspects of dialysis. The primary nurse must still take responsibility to reinforce and answer all relevant questions related to this treatment option. This knowledge will not only answer the patient and family questions,, it will let them know that you are a content expert and that they are in good hands! This is a caring intervention when the nurse explains and teaches what is needed well!

To effectively educate patients and family, the nurse must emphasize both SIMPLICITY and REINFORCEMENT.
Simplicity
- *Teach simple concepts about a topic first, and then move to the more complex concepts.*
- *Use language that your patient will find easy to understand and avoid medical terminology whenever possible. Consider the age, level of education, and current profession to determine the level at which to teach (Freda, 2004).*

Reinforcement
- *Teach the one concept you want your patient to learn FIRST.*
- *Ask your patient to restate what you have taught, so you can be sure he understood.*
- *Use visual aids for teaching; using several senses improves learning.*
- *Always use written educational materials for the client to take home, if available (Freda, 2004).*

Additional principles that I have found helpful to promote patient engagement and meaningful learning:
- *Define the priority educational needs and desired outcome of education.*
- *Minimize any/all distractions and teach at a time that is best for the patient.*

Encourage and support the wife and any family members throughout this process of education and treatment decisions. When communication is open, though difficult, there can be peace in the midst of a storm!

6. What is the expected response of the patient that indicate the nursing interventions were effective?
Both patient and family would be able to verbally restate the current dilemma and accurately identify the pros and cons of medical management vs. dialysis.

In essence, what the nurse looks for is acceptance by the patient that he is clearly convinced of his choice and right to autonomy, as well as acceptance by the spouse regarding the husband's right to make this decision whatever it may be.

7. What response by the patient would indicate that a change in the plan of care and nursing interventions are needed?
If the patient was clearly hesitant or uncertain of the best option e or anything that would demonstrate a lack of clear understanding would need to be investigated. If the wife does not accept and continues to verbalize her desires regardless of what her husband wants, this, too, would be a clinical red flag.

8. What is the patient and/or family likely experiencing/feeling right now in this situation?
Though the patient is dying and will face death sooner if he does not pursue aggressive medical management, there is no data to determine if he has spiritual concerns related to death and dying. This needs to be assumed by the nurse and may need exploration by the nurse or with the chaplain.

The wife is clearly conflicted and is struggling with his current change in health. She will need additional support. By using open-ended questions the essence of how she is processing this situation and will help the team determine the level of outside support needed.

9. What can I do to engage myself with this patient's experience, and show that she matters to me as a person?
The essence of empathy is to put one's self in the shoes of person you are caring for or the family and gauge their response. If the nurse can consciously make this transition, it becomes much easier to be moved with a heart of compassion for those that one cares for.

Swanson (1991) identified the following caring interventions in the practice setting that have relevance in this scenario to engage with this patient's experience and support the patient and family in this crisis:

Family caring interventions
- *Maintain a hope-filled attitude*
- *Offer realistic optimism*
- *Support the family*
- *Explain all that is taking place and answer any/all questions*
- *Convey availability to the family*

Patient caring interventions
- *Preserve the dignity of the patient*
- *Anticipate needs*
- *Comfort the patient in any way*
- *Seek cues by paying close attention to the patient's response and anticipate her expected response*
- *Perform competently and skillfully as a nurse. This communicates caring to your patient!*
- *Convey availability to the patient*

10. What was learned from this case study that you will incorporate into your practice?
Content knowledge without personal application will not be fruitful. Reflection is an essential professional behavior that can also be practiced! I have added this question to allow students to intentionally reflect on what they have learned so that they can integrate this essential content into their practice and fully develop the ethical comportment of the professional nurse. This question will facilitate rich dialogue in whatever context you choose to use this case study. If there is not enough time to discuss this question, consider having students write a one-page reflection paper.

References

Dameron, C.M. (2005). Spiritual assessment made easy...With acronyms! Journal of Christian Nursing, 22, 14-16.

Freda, M. (2004). Issues in patient education. Journal of Midwifery & Woman's Health, retrieved from http://www.medscape.com/viewarticle/478283_3

Levett-Jones, T., Hoffman, K., Dempsey, J., Yeun-Sim Jeong, S., Noble, D., Norton, C. Hickey, N. (2010). The 'five rights' of clinical reasoning: An educational model to enhance nursing students' ability to identify and manage clinically 'at risk' patients. *Nurse Education Today,* 30, 515–520.

Swanson, K. M. (1991). Empirical development of a middle range theory of caring. *Nursing Research, 40*(3), 161–166.

Wright, L. & Leahey, M. (1999). Maximizing time, minimizing suffering: The 15-minute (or less) family interview. Journal of Family Nursing, 5(3), 259-274.

TREATMENT Dilemma

Left Ventricular Assist Device (LVAD) or Hospice

STUDENT Worksheet

Mabel Anderson, 70 years old

Overview

Though aggressive medical management is expected with a patient who is critically ill, there comes a time when the paths of quality of life and quantity of life intersect and the patient must make a choice. A newer treatment option for end stage heart failure is a left ventricular assist device (LVAD). Though it can prolong life, it requires an external battery pack and other limitations that impact the quality of daily life. How the nurse can care and support a patient who is facing this decision and has a fear of dying is the essence of this treatment dilemma.

Left Ventricular Assist Device (LVAD) or Hospice

I. Contextualizing the Dilemma

History of Present Problem:

Mabel Anderson is a 70-year-old woman who has a history of coronary artery disease, chronic renal insufficiency, atrial fibrillation, ischemic cardiomyopathy, and systolic heart failure with an ejection fraction of 10-15%. She has gained 12 pounds in the last four days. She has had increased shortness of breath (SOB) the past two days and was unable to sleep lying flat yesterday, but slept in her recliner instead. Upon awakening this morning she was SOB and brought to the ED by paramedics. She was admitted to the ICU where she had a Swan-Ganz pulmonary artery catheter placed and started on furosemide and dobutamine IV continuous drips. This is her third admission for heart failure in the past two months.

Personal/Social History:

Mabel just celebrated her 50th wedding anniversary and is happily married to her husband, John. They have no children due to her struggles with infertility. Mabel has not attended church for the past forty years, though she grew up in the Lutheran church.

What data from the histories is important & RELEVANT; therefore it has clinical significance to the nurse?

RELEVANT Data from Present Problem:	Clinical Significance:
RELEVANT Data from Social History:	Clinical Significance:

II. The Dilemma Begins...

Current Concern:

Two days after being admitted, Mabel has lost 3.5 kg due to diuresis. She remains on the furosemide IV drip at 20 mg/hour and dobutamine is at 5 mcg/kg. Her cardiac output is currently 3.1 and her cardiac index is 1.5. Her pulmonary wedge pressure is 24 (12 hours ago was 28) and her central venous pressure is 14 (12 hours ago was 18). She is no longer SOB, but appears depressed with a flat affect.

The cardiologist has communicated Mabel has only months to live with medical management. He has suggested that she may be a candidate for a permanent left ventricular assist device (LVAD) that would be a motor surgically implanted in her upper abdomen that would assist her failing heart and improve cardiac output. It requires an external battery life pack that she would have to carry with her the rest of her life. Though this option may prolong her life, Mabel is clearly ambivalent about this option. After the cardiologist has left she replies to the nurse, "I am fearful of dying, but I don't want to live like that!"

What data from the current concern is important & RELEVANT; therefore it has clinical significance to the nurse?

RELEVANT Data from Current Concern:	Clinical Significance:

III. Resolving the Dilemma

1. *Identifying data that is RELEVANT, what is the essence of this current dilemma?*

2. *What additional information is needed by the nurse that would help clarify the current dilemma?*

3. *What additional members of the healthcare team could be used in this situation? Why?*

4. *What is the nursing priority?*

5. *What nursing interventions and/or principles can the nurse use to successfully resolve this clinical dilemma?*

6. *What is the expected response of the patient that indicate the nursing interventions were effective?*

7. *What response by the patient would indicate that a change in the plan of care and nursing interventions are needed?*

8. *What is the patient and/or family likely experiencing/feeling right now in this situation?*

9. *What can I do to engage myself with this patient's experience, and show that she matters to me as a person?*

10. *What was learned from this case study that you will incorporate into your practice?*

TREATMENT Dilemma

Left Ventricular Assist Device (LVAD) or Hospice

Mabel Anderson, 70 years old

Answer Key

Clinical Dilemma Activity: ANSWER KEY

Left Ventricular Assist Device (LVAD) or Hospice

I. Contextualizing the Dilemma

History of Present Problem:

Mabel Anderson is a 70-year-old woman who has a history of coronary artery disease, chronic renal insufficiency, atrial fibrillation, ischemic cardiomyopathy, and systolic heart failure with an ejection fraction of 10-15%. She has gained 12 pounds in the last four days. She has had increased shortness of breath (SOB) the past two days and was unable to sleep lying flat yesterday, but slept in her recliner instead. Upon awakening this morning she was SOB and brought to the ED by paramedics. She was admitted to the ICU where she had a Swan-Ganz pulmonary artery catheter placed and started on furosemide and dobutamine IV continuous drips. This is her third admission for heart failure in the past two months.

Personal/Social History:

Mabel just celebrated her 50th wedding anniversary and is happily married to her husband, John. They have no children due to her struggles with infertility. Mabel has not attended church for the past forty years, though she grew up in the Lutheran church.

What data from the histories is important & RELEVANT; therefore it has clinical significance to the nurse?

RELEVANT Data from Present Problem:	Clinical Significance:
70 year-old woman who has a history of coronary artery disease, chronic renal insufficiency, atrial fibrillation, ischemic cardiomyopathy, and systolic heart failure with an ejection fraction of 10-15%.	*Though these case studies emphasize the art of nursing, the nurse must also integrate knowledge of the applied sciences and content from the classroom to every patient encounter.* *The age of the patient is always relevant. Though she is 70 and elderly, the average life expectancy of women in the US is 81, so she is below this average. The older the patient, the more likely they are to experience higher rates of complications with any procedures. Of the five rights of clinical reasoning, the "right" patient must always be considered as one who may be at higher risk for an adverse outcome because of age or other factors such as altered immune status or chronic illnesses (Levett–Jones et al., 2010).* *An important component of thinking like a nurse is the ability to identify relationships of clinical data. In the context of Mabel's medical problems, it is important for the nurse to recognize that this cluster of medical problems did not develop in isolation. Each one of these illnesses have relationship to the other. They are like dominos that begin to fall. When one starts, the other problems develop as a result. Her coronary artery disease was likely responsible for causing the development of the ischemic cardiomyopathy that led to end-stage heart failure with an ejection fraction (EF) of only 10 to 15%. As a result of the poor perfusion to the kidneys, Mabel has developed chronic renal insufficiency and impaired kidney function. This is not uncommon with many patients who have heart failure.* *10-15% ejection fraction is END STAGE heart failure and approaching incompatibility with life. Review normal EF (60-65%) and how low this is from a normal heart. Have students explain in their own words what ejection fraction is to ensure that they truly understand this concept and content.*
She has gained 12 pounds in the last four days. She has had increased shortness of breath (SOB) the past two days and was	*This cluster of data is suggesting a significant exacerbation of heart failure. To gain 12 pounds of weight in only four days is extremely high and the expected shortness of breath and inability to lie flat reflect left-*

© 2015 Keith Rischer/www.KeithRN.com

76

unable to sleep lying flat yesterday, but slept in her recliner instead.	*sided to right-sided heart failure.*
Upon awakening this morning she was SOB and brought to the ED by paramedics. She was admitted to the ICU where she had a Swan-Ganz pulmonary artery catheter placed and started on furosemide and dobutamine IV continuous drips.	*If a hospital has the ability to place a Swan-Ganz pulmonary artery catheter, this intervention will conclusively identify the severity of her right-sided or fluid volume status regarding preload as well as the left ventricular and diastolic pressure measured by the wedge pressure (left-sided preload). In the context of an acute exacerbation of heart failure, the nurse must have a deep understanding of the pathophysiology of heart failure as well as the importance of furosemide and dobutamine as continuous intravenous medications. How will these medications benefit a patient in acute biventricular heart failure? Be sure that your students have this foundational knowledge of heart failure management before proceeding further in this case study!*
This is her third admission for heart failure in the past two months.	*Heart failure exacerbation is one of the most common reasons for readmission for the elderly. Though readmission is not uncommon for a patient with heart failure, to have three admissions for the same problem in the past two months reflects an unstable heart failure patient who needs more effective management of this problem.*
RELEVANT Data from Social History:	**Clinical Significance:**
Mabel just celebrated her 50th wedding anniversary and is happily married to her husband John.	*Though this information may not seem at first glance relevant, knowing that Mabel has essential psychosocial support is important to note especially as it relates to discharge planning. In addition to the patient, the husband must be included in all patient education. The nurse must ensure that the patient and her husband have a deep understanding of the most important concepts related to her heart failure.*
They have no children due to her struggles with infertility.	*Though this may not seem significant when combined with what is noted in the chart regarding her lack of church involvement, Mabel may have some spiritual concerns that she may want to address as she is approaches end of life.*
Mabel has not attended church for the past forty years, though she grew up in the Lutheran church.	*Though church is not important to every patient, when a patient has been active in church but is no longer, there may be a reason for this. Noting her infertility struggles, there may be a relationship, but it is not the responsibility of the nurse in this context to explore this. It may be best for a chaplain to be consulted if the patient is willing.*

II. The Dilemma Begins...

Current Concern:

Two days after being admitted, Mabel has lost 3.5 kg due to diuresis. She remains on the furosemide IV drip at 20 mg/hour and dobutamine is at 5 mcg/kg. Her cardiac output is currently 3.1 and her cardiac index is 1.5. Her pulmonary wedge pressure is 24 (12 hours ago was 28) and her central venous pressure is 14 (12 hours ago was 18). She is no longer SOB, but appears depressed with a flat affect.

The cardiologist has communicated to Mabel that she has only months to live with medical management. He has suggested that she may be a candidate for a permanent left ventricular assist device (LVAD) that would be a motor surgically implanted in her upper abdomen. It would assist her failing heart and improve cardiac output. It requires an external battery life pack that she would have to carry with her the rest of her life. Though this option may prolong her life, Mabel is clearly ambivalent about this option. After the cardiologist has left, she replies to the nurse, "I am fearful of dying, but I don't want to live like that!"

What data from the current concern is important & RELEVANT; therefore it has clinical significance to the nurse?

RELEVANT Data from Current Concern:	Clinical Significance:
Mabel has lost 3.5 kg due to diuresis. She remains on the furosemide IV drip at 20 mg/hour and dobutamine is at 5 mcg/kg.	*Remember that 3.5 kg equals 3500 mL of volume! This is almost a gallon of urine output. This is a good thing because she was in acute exacerbation of heart failure but ask students what also is lost with excessive diuresis? The essential electrolytes of potassium, magnesium, and sodium. Of these three electrolytes, potassium is depleted most quickly and is also one of the most important because of its relevance to electrical cardiac function. This is be a good time to review the signs of hypokalemia and emphasize its relevance in this clinical context.*
Her cardiac output is currently 3.1 and her cardiac index is 1.5. Her pulmonary wedge pressure is 24 (12 hours ago was 28) and her central venous pressure is 14 (12 hours ago was 18).	*This content is an excellent review for advanced med/surgical students. In order to recognize if these numbers are cause for concern, the normal ranges must be noted. When it is known that a normal cardiac output is 4-8 liters, normal cardiac index is 2 to 4, normal wedge pressure is 8 to 12, and a normal CVP is 2-6, this data must be deeply understood and its relevance to overall cardiac function recognized.* *It is readily apparent that Mabel has a poorly functioning heart with an elevated left-sided pressure as well as right-sided pressure. Though she has lost almost 4 liters, these numbers reflect that there is still more fluid to give.* *This is also an excellent opportunity to compare and contrast textbook norms to patient norms, even when the patient gets to their baseline. Because of a weakened heart, Mabel will never have textbook numbers relating to cardiac output. Her normal, when she is clinically stable, will likely be higher filling pressures (both CVP and wedge) in order to have adequate cardiac output. Remember Starling's Law? This is an excellent time to situate this pathophysiologic concept to clinical practice!*
She is no longer SOB, but appears depressed with a flat affect.	*Physiologically, Mabel is improving. She is no longer short of breath and in acute exacerbation of heart failure. But she appears depressed and is nonverbally communicating this with a flat affect. The astute nurse must always ask why with regard to what motivates any physiologic, emotional, or spiritual needs that a patient may have. Recognizing that Mabel is obviously depressed, this observation must not be ignored, but explored with an appropriate open ended therapeutic question.* *The nurse must always be aware that, though the physiologic needs of the patient are the initial highest priority and the most obvious reason that a patient comes to the hospital, the impact of any physiologic illness to the spirit and the soul of the patient must always be considered.*
The cardiologist has communicated to Mabel that she has only months to live with medical management.	*This communication from the cardiologist is the most obvious reason that Mabel is depressed. End-stage heart failure is equivalent to terminal cancer. There comes a time when there is nothing more that can be done by medical management. Mabel has reached this point, which will likely result in numerous emotional and spiritual concerns. She has many upcoming decisions that could include hospice care as an option.*

He has suggested that she may be a candidate for a permanent left ventricular assist device (LVAD) that would be a motor surgically implanted in her upper abdomen that would assist her failing heart and improve cardiac output.	When medical management has been exhausted, an LVAD can be a viable option and appropriate destination therapy for those patients who are willing to be compliant and accepting of its use as well as limitations.
It requires an external battery life pack that she would have to carry with her the rest of her life.	One of the most obvious physical limitations is that this device is not completely internal like a pacemaker. Though the motor that supports the heart is internal, it requires an external battery power source. The patient has a responsibility to ensure that the power source is always connected and maintained.
Though this option may prolong her life, Mabel is clearly ambivalent about this option. After the cardiologist has left she replies to the nurse, "I am fearful of dying, but I don't want to live like that!"	It is not uncommon for many patients to have reservations about their willingness to have an LVAD. Just like other life-altering treatment options like dialysis, it is important for the patient to carefully consider all the options and make a decision that they can truly live with. Because Mabel has a terminal prognosis without this therapy, she understands that she is dying. Her fear of dying must not be taken lightly but is something that needs to be explored at some point soon. Though she has not been active in her church for many years, it would be appropriate for the nurse to ask permission to obtain a referral for a chaplain or to support her in that moment if he/she is comfortable doing so.

III. Resolving the Dilemma

1. Identifying data that is RELEVANT, what is the essence of this current dilemma?

Mabel has reached the terminal stage of heart failure and can no longer be successfully medically managed. She has to choose between ongoing medical management which will lead to death shortly, or pursue a more invasive and life-altering treatment option of an LVAD to prolong her life. She is also expressing feelings related to spiritual distress because of a fear of dying yet not wanting to live with an LVAD.

Mabel also expressed she has been away from church for 40 years. Many times there is significant guilt surrounding this issue. The nurse might consider a response to relieve the guilt and refocus the conversation on taking action. "The clergy/God is waiting for you." Sometimes this will open the conversation to encourage the patient to be open to spiritual interventions.

When patients struggle physically and emotionally, the primary strength that can be depended on is spirituality. It is like a three-legged stool representing the physical, affective and spiritual domains within each of us. If two legs of the stool are weakened with the current patient crisis, the patient frequently is open to spiritual intervention if it is handled in a sensitive manner. This patient is experiencing this crisis physically and emotionally. Forty years of being absent from church is an obstacle for her.

2. What additional information is needed by the nurse that would help clarify the current dilemma?

The nurse must advocate for Mabel by ensuring that she and her husband completely and clearly understand all aspects and implications of both treatment options. Are they able to restate in their own words the most important aspects of both treatment options?

Does the patient have a voice, and has she clearly communicated what she would want regarding treatment options? If there is conflict in the family over the best option, it is essential to establish a trust relationship with the patient so that they can comfortably share in private what they really want. Not what the children want, or with the husband may want, but what the patient wants. This is the essence of autonomy, and Mabel's desires must be clearly identified and communicated to the treatment team.

Does Mabel have any spiritual concerns? This patient is at the end of life and spiritual issues often surface at this point though they may not be readily apparent. Spiritual assessment for this patient might be explored with the FICA acronym. This model is useful for any faith belief system. FICA acronym represents:

- ***F-Faith or beliefs:*** *What are your spiritual beliefs? Do you consider yourself spiritual? What things do you believe in that give meaning to life?*
- ***I-Importance and influence:*** *Is faith important to you? How has your illness or hospitalization affected your personal belief practices?*
- ***C-Community:*** *Are you connected to a faith center in the community? Does it provide support/comfort for you during times of stress? Is there a person/group who assists you in your spirituality?*
- ***A-Address:*** *What can I do for you? What support can health care provide to support your spiritual beliefs/practices? (Dameron, 2005).*

These questions, if used in this scenario by the nurse, would naturally explore this patient's spirituality. It is always best if the nurse has some comfort with the exploration of spirituality. Patients can sense discomfort or anxiety in approaching this portion of the assessment. The FICA model offers some open-ended questions to make spiritual assessment a natural part of the conversation. Use this spiritual assessment tool to make caring for the spirit an essential component of your nursing practice!

3. What additional members of the healthcare team could be used in this situation? Why?
- ***Chaplain.*** *Whenever there are issues of death and dying, it is essential to have this input.*
- ***Social services.*** *If Mabel chooses to have the LVAD, it will require numerous discharge and care priorities that must be considered. This input is also essential.*
- ***Cardiologist or nurse practitioner of the cardiologist.*** *Though they are already involved, education and complete understanding is essential. Usually this lengthier education is initially done by the cardiologist's nurse practitioner. Do not hesitate to have them come back and explain any aspects that the nurse may discern are not completely understood by the patient or family. Better yet, the primary nurse must also be able to answer general questions related to LVAD.*
- ***Case manager.*** *If the patient transitions to another level of care, the case manager will be involved and can be included in presenting options to the patient. Frequently, the case manager is a nurse who knows the community resources and can help the patient access them.*

4. What is the nursing priority?
The following NANDA nursing diagnostic statements are relevant and appropriate for this scenario:
- *Knowledge deficit*
- *Spiritual distress*
- *Anxiety*
- *Disturbed body image*
- *Fear*
- *Hopelessness*
- *Powerlessness*

5. What nursing interventions and/or principles can the nurse use to successfully resolve this clinical dilemma?
Though there are numerous potential nursing priorities that could be considered in this scenario, the essence centers on knowledge deficit and spiritual distress.

Knowledge deficit
In this scenario, though the nurse practitioner or specialty educator will be responsible for primary education, it is important that the primary nurse has a strong working knowledge of all aspects of the LVAD device. The primary nurse must still take responsibility to reinforce and answer all relevant questions related to this treatment option. This knowledge will not only answer questions by the patient and family that will support the patient, but knowing that you are a content expert will also demonstrate that they are in good hands! This is in essence a caring intervention when the nurse explains and teaches what is needed well!

To effectively educate patients and family, the nurse must emphasize both SIMPLICITY and REINFORCEMENT.

Simplicity
- Teach simple concepts about a topic first, and then move to the more complex concepts.
- Use language that your patient will find easy to understand and avoid medical terminology whenever possible. Consider the age, level of education, and current profession to determine the level at which to teach (Freda, 2004).

Reinforcement
- Teach the one concept you want your patient to learn FIRST.
- Ask your patient to restate what you have taught, so you can be sure they understand.
- Another way to clarify what the patient is thinking is "I heard you say...does that mean/indicate_____? Tell me more about_____,"
- Use visual aids for teaching; using several senses improves learning.
- Always use written educational materials for the client to take home, if available (Freda, 2004).
- Focus and listen to the patient to sort out what the patient NEEDS to know from what is NICE to know. The priority teaching needs are the NEED to know. Listen and focus your teaching on the patient priority.

Additional principles that I have found helpful to promote patient engagement and meaningful learning include the following:
- Define the priority educational needs and desired outcome of education.
- Minimize any/all distractions and teach at a time that is best for the patient.
- Include the FAMILY as much as possible in education. The spouse or significant other will be needed to reinforce your teaching once the patient is home.

Spiritual distress
Because of concerns about death and dying, the following nursing interventions are relevant and appropriate in this scenario:

Nurse presence.
When the nurse is present and with the patient in a non-hurried manner, this clearly communicates the caring and support that Mabel needs at this time. Presence for the nurse is being present in the moment with the patient and his moment which is happening **now**. The emotional breakthroughs don't last long but are critical for nurses to connect with the patient. Patients sense whether the nurse is willing to "go there" or not. If they sense you are not willing to be in the moment with them, they will pull back and the moment ends. If the nurse fiddles with the computer or indicates nonverbally a discomfort with what is happening, it will decrease trust with the nurse.

Patients don't care how much you know until they know how much you care. This is about focusing on the patient and giving caring responses to build trust. It truly is a privilege for the nurse to have a patient share the "tough stuff" in life with you. Generally, the patient will not share like this unless they trust you or they are in an affective domain crisis.

Silence.
There are situations where no words are needed. Sitting in silence with a patient in this context does not need to be awkward but indirectly communicates presence as well as caring. Pauses can be productive. They allow patients to process what is happening to them. After the silence, be willing to listen and go where the patient takes you.

Touch.
Reaching out and touching the patient's hand or shoulder and assessing the response to this intervention would also communicate caring and support in this scenario. One cannot know how a patient will receive touch, so the nurse must first assess the patient response. If the nurse allows the patient in control to withdraw touch, it simplifies evaluation of the intervention of touch. One simple way to implement this approach is to slip your hand under the patient's hand with your palm up. The patient can withdraw their hand at any time if the nurse's hand is not on top of the patient's hand and provides needed control for the patient.

Open-ended spiritual assessment questions.
There are a number of questions that the nurse can select from to ask a patient in spiritual crisis. At times asking one question will open up the conversation and the patient will begin to share openly.

    o *Are you connected with a faith community?*
    o *What is your source of strength, peace, faith, hope, and worth?*
    o *What spiritual practices are important to you?*
    o *What can I do to support your faith?*
    o *What makes life meaningful for you?*
    o *What do you feel is the meaning of all that you are currently experiencing?*

Though each of these questions are effective tools to make a quick spiritual assessment for most patients, in this scenario most of these questions are not relevant because Mabel does not have a faith community that she identifies with. But there is one question that should be considered: what is your source of strength or peace? She may have some personal strategies or approaches that she has drawn upon in the past..

6. What is the expected response of the patient that indicate the nursing interventions were effective?
Knowledge deficit
Both patient and family are able to verbally restate the most important aspects related to the treatment option of LVAD

Spiritual distress
- *Patient is visibly calm, relaxed, and less anxious*
- *Patient may verbalize her feelings and how she is feeling in the present that indicates that she is resolving her fear of death*
- *Patient is willing to meet with a chaplain*

7. What response by the patient would indicate that a change in the plan of care and nursing interventions are needed?
If Mabel continues to be visibly anxious, depressed with a flat affect, or other signs that she is not engaged in her current care and is demonstrating the inability to make a decision that is reflective of her wishes and desires. Though it will take time to work through these significant and life-changing matters, the nurse must step back and see the direction is the patient moving toward. Is it obvious that acceptance and making a choice that she would want to pursue is evident, or is she continuing to struggle and communicate ongoing fear, anxiety, or distress?

8. What is the patient and/or family likely experiencing/feeling right now in this situation?
Though the patient is dying and will face death sooner if she does not pursue aggressive medical management, she has expressed some fear of dying which needs further exploration. It is also important to recognize that Mabel is likely TIRED and frustrated regarding her deteriorating medical condition. It is not uncommon for some to look forward to death as a blessing if there is a hope for eternal spiritual rest.

The husband's response and experience is unknown but it is likely that he is experiencing feelings of loss and grieving the loss of his best friend. Because they have no children, these feelings of loss will likely be even stronger.

9. What can I do to engage myself with this patient's experience, and show that she matters to me as a person?
The essence of empathy is to put oneself in the shoes of those you are caring for or the family and how they are responding. If the nurse can consciously make this transition, it becomes much easier to be moved with a heart of compassion for those that one cares for.

Swanson (1991) identified the following caring interventions in the practice setting that have relevance in this scenario to engage with this patient's experience and support both the patient and family in this crisis:

Family caring interventions
- *Maintain a hope filled attitude*
- *Offer realistic optimism*
- *Support the family*
- *Explain all that is taking place and answer any/all questions*

- *Convey availability to the family*

Patient caring interventions
- *Preserve the dignity of the patient*
- *Anticipate needs*
- *Comfort the patient in any way*
- *Seek cues by paying close attention to the patient's response and anticipate her expected response*
- *Perform competently and skillfully as a nurse. This communicates caring to your patient!*
- *Convey availability to the patient*

10. What was learned from this case study that you will incorporate into your practice?
Content knowledge without personal application will not be fruitful. Reflection is an essential professional behavior that can also be practiced! I have added this question to allow students to intentionally reflect on what they have learned so that they can integrate this essential content into their practice and fully develop the ethical comportment of the professional nurse. This question will facilitate rich dialogue in whatever context you choose to use this case study. If there is not enough time to discuss this question, consider having students write a one-page reflection paper.

References

Dameron, C.M. (2005). Spiritual assessment made easy…With acronyms! Journal of Christian Nursing, 22, 14-16.

Freda, M. (2004). Issues in patient education. Journal of Midwifery & Woman's Health, retrieved from http://www.medscape.com/viewarticle/478283_3

Levett-Jones, T., Hoffman, K., Dempsey, J., Yeun-Sim Jeong, S., Noble, D., Norton, C. Hickey, N. (2010). The 'five rights' of clinical reasoning: An educational model to enhance nursing students' ability to identify and manage clinically 'at risk' patients. Nurse Education Today, 30, 515–520.

Swanson, K. M. (1991). Empirical development of a middle range theory of caring. *Nursing Research, 40*(3), 161–166.

TREATMENT Dilemma

Transitioning to Comfort Care

STUDENT Worksheet

John Peterson, 75 years old

Overview

Death is inevitable. When it becomes apparent that aggressive medical treatment is no longer a treatment option, it is not uncommon to find that some members of the family cannot accept this grim prognosis, but insist that everything that can be done must be done. How can the nurse support both the patient and a grieving family is the essence of this dilemma.

Clinical Dilemma Activity: STUDENT

Transitioning to Comfort Care

I. Scenario

History of Present Problem:

John Peterson is a 75-year-old who has a history of ischemic cardiomyopathy with an ejection fraction of 20%, atrial fibrillation, mitral regurgitation and chronic kidney disease. He has been hospitalized three times in the last two months for heart failure exacerbation. He was admitted two weeks ago for SOB and heart failure exacerbation and has been aggressively managed in the ICU with furosemide, dopamine, and dobutamine intravenous drips. His creatinine has risen from 1.8 to 2.7 in the last 24 hours. John is not a surgical candidate to repair his mitral valve that is contributing to his need for hospitalization.

John has openly expressed his desire to family members that he wants to stop all treatment and that he just wants to die. The physician changed his code status from full code to DNR-DNI but did not stop all other supportive therapies. When the oldest son, Steve, arrives later that day and finds out that his code status has been changed to DNR-DNI, he becomes angry and insists that it is too soon to give up. He pulls Ruth, the primary nurse aside and tells her, "Nobody asked me about this. I insist that you call the doctor and change this!"

Personal/Social History:

John has been married for 52 years and has a son and daughter. The family is consistently present in John's room and at his bedside. His wife and younger daughter are in agreement with John's desire to have his code status changed to DNR/DNI but are not willing to withdraw medical treatment and support. They feel he is not thinking clearly and may be delirious from his illness so they insist that everything continue to be done.

What data from the histories is important & RELEVANT; therefore it has clinical significance to the nurse?

RELEVANT Data from Present Problem:	Clinical Significance:

RELEVANT Data from Social History:	Clinical Significance:

II. The Dilemma Begins...

Current Concern:

After Steve's angry outburst, the nurse communicates to the primary provider that a care conference needs to be scheduled as soon as possible. Two days later, the care conference took place and all of John's family was in attendance as well as the medical treatment team. The grim prognosis of his current status was presented and all questions were answered by the treatment team. Steve, the oldest son, asks numerous questions. John continues to insist that he wants all treatments stopped and just wants to die. After the care conference, there is a consensus between the family and treatment team to stop all supportive therapies including intravenous drips and most scheduled medications and place John on comfort care in addition to his DNR/DNI code status.

After the care conference, the nurse discontinues all intravenous drips and John is transferred to the medical floor where he will be allowed to die.

What data from the current concern is important & RELEVANT; therefore it has clinical significance to the nurse?

RELEVANT Data from Current Concern:	Clinical Significance:

III. Resolving the Dilemma

1. Identifying data that is RELEVANT, what is the essence of this current dilemma?

2. What additional information is needed by the nurse that would help clarify the current dilemma?

3. What additional members of the healthcare team could be utilized in this situation? Why?

4. What is the nursing priority?

5. What nursing interventions and/or principles can be utilized by the nurse to successfully resolve this clinical dilemma?

6. What is the expected response of the patient that indicate the nursing interventions were effective?

7. What response by the patient would indicate that a change in the plan of care and nursing interventions are needed?

8. What is the patient and/or family likely experiencing/feeling right now in this situation?

9. What can I do to engage myself with this patient's experience, and show that he/she matters to me as a person?

10. What was learned from this case study that you will incorporate into your practice?

TREATMENT Dilemma
Transitioning to Comfort Care

John Peterson, 75 years old

Answer Key

Clinical Dilemma Activity: ANSWER KEY

Transitioning to Comfort Care

I. Scenario

History of Present Problem:

John Peterson is a 75-year-old who has a history of ischemic cardiomyopathy with an ejection fraction of 20%, atrial fibrillation, mitral regurgitation and chronic kidney disease. He has been hospitalized three times in the last two months for heart failure exacerbation. He was admitted two weeks ago for SOB and heart failure exacerbation and has been aggressively managed in the ICU with furosemide, dopamine, and dobutamine intravenous drips. His creatinine has risen from 1.8 to 2.7 in the last 24 hours. John is not a surgical candidate to repair his mitral valve that is contributing to his need for hospitalization.

John has openly expressed his desire to family members that he wants to stop all treatment and that he just wants to die. The physician changed his code status from full code to DNR-DNI but did not stop all other supportive therapies. When the oldest son, Steve, arrives later that day and finds out that his code status has been changed to DNR-DNI, he becomes angry and insists that it is too soon to give up. He pulls Ruth, the primary nurse aside and tells her, "Nobody asked me about this. I insist that you call the doctor and change this!"

Personal/Social History:

John has been married for 52 years and has a son and daughter. The family is consistently present in John's room and at his bedside. His wife and younger daughter are in agreement with John's desire to have his code status changed to DNR/DNI but are not willing to withdraw medical treatment and support. They feel he is not thinking clearly and may be delirious from his illness so they insist that everything continue to be done.

What data from the histories is important & RELEVANT; therefore it has clinical significance to the nurse?

RELEVANT Data from Present Problem:	Clinical Significance:
John Peterson is a 75-year-old who has a history of ischemic cardiomyopathy with an ejection fraction of 20%, atrial fibrillation, mitral regurgitation and chronic kidney disease.	*John has three chronic diseases and each is potentially fatal. With a 20% ejection fraction, this directly impacts the quality of life because typically any activity that translates beyond sitting in a chair will produce exertional dyspnea.*
He has been hospitalized three times in the last two months for heart failure exacerbation. He was admitted two weeks ago for SOB and heart failure exacerbation.	*Heart failure is the most common reason for hospital readmissions in the United States. As heart failure approaches end stage it becomes increasingly difficult to manage. Imagine a narrow balance beam that represents medical treatment. It is possible to walk slowly on the beam and remain clinically stable, but retain a little too much fluid, and this will cause the patient to lose balance, become SOB and fall off the balance beam!*
Has been aggressively managed in the ICU with furosemide, dopamine, and dobutamine intravenous drips.	*Having this many hospital readmissions in a short time frame is a clinical RED FLAG that John's heart failure is becoming more difficult to manage and is "falling off the beam" as a result.*
His creatinine has risen from 1.8 to 2.7 in the last 24 hours. John is not a surgical candidate to repair his mitral valve that is contributing to his worsening of heart failure.	*The fact that he remains managed with these drips for two weeks indicates he is dependent on them to maintain perfusion to vital organs. ICU is the only place this drug combination can be managed and titrated to his physiological needs.*
John has openly expressed his desire to stop all treatment and that he just wants to die.	*Despite aggressive medical management, he has renal failure and inadequate perfusion to his kidneys with no options to correct the underlying heart problem. We are at the end of the line with options for this patient.*

The physician changed his code status from full code to DNR-DNI but did not stop all other supportive therapies.	John has made his wishes known to stop all treatment. John's wishes should be honored and be documented if he remains competent to make decisions.
When the oldest son Steve arrives later that day and finds out that his code status has been changed to DNR-DNI, he becomes angry and insists that it is too soon to give up.	The nurse needs to encourage that an advanced directive be written or produced. Why did the physician chose to change the code status but "not stop all other supportive therapies?" The nurse might question the plan for the current supportive therapies and discuss with the patient how he feels about this. The nurse can advocate for the patient's wishes if the patient wants the entire drug regimen stopped and be allowed to die.

Steve does not have the authority to make a decision about his father's code status, and this request must not be honored. Steve will be the one who has to live with the guilt when his father dies. The nurse must choose NOT to react to the anger and take it personally, but step back and choose to see this experience from Steve's perspective. This is the essence of empathy and is needed so that the nurse remains engaged in this difficult situation. It is all too easy and quite common in practice to see nurses respond to the emotion and label the family or the patient as a "problem." The nurse needs to empathize and realize Steve's perspective and should help him work through his feelings by asking open-ended questions. For example, the most obvious question to ask in this scenario is when did Steve last see his father? According to the chart, it has been two years. |
| He pulls Ruth, the primary nurse aside and tells her, "Nobody asked me about this. I insist that you call the doctor and change this!" | Just as the nurse must make it a priority to educate the patient in a situation such as this, the importance of educating the entire family of all aspects of his heart failure, his treatment,, and his poor response to all that can be done to support his heart at this time.

Communication is a priority between the family and care providers. Do all that is possible to ensure that all that can be done to facilitate this is done. |

RELEVANT Data from Social History:	**Clinical Significance:**
John has been married for 52 years and has a son and daughter. The family is consistently present in John's room and at his bedside. His wife and younger daughter are in agreement with John's desire to have his code status changed to DNR/DNI	This is a functional family unit, but it is not unusual for families to have each member on a different page when facing the end of life of one of the members. Different people process at different rates and in different ways. It is not surprising that one of them is having difficulty dealing with this situation. This family has a lot of strengths to help them through this event that may not be evident to the nurse. It must be remembered that Steve is his son and the passing of his father will put Steve in a new role. Depending on their father/son relationship, this alters life permanently. An observant nurse can detect the father/son relationship and realize what this loss means to Steve.
But are not willing to withdraw medical treatment and support. They do not feel he is thinking clearly and may be delirious from his illness so they insist that everything continue to be done.	This is not uncommon in clinical practice. A patient who is competent becomes critically ill. The patient expresses his desire to die. The family assumes he does not really mean it because he is delirious due to the length of time he has been in ICU. This ironically may be true, but it also may not be the case and the wishes of the patient must be honored.

II. The Dilemma Begins…

Current Concern:

After Steve's angry outburst, the nurse communicates to the primary provider that a care conference needs to be scheduled as soon as possible. Two days later, the care conference took place and all of John's family was in attendance as well as the medical treatment team. The grim prognosis of his current status was presented and all questions were answered by the treatment team. Steve, the oldest son, asks numerous questions. John continues to insist that he wants all treatments stopped and just wants to die. After the care conference, there is a consensus between the family and treatment team to stop all supportive therapies including intravenous dripsand most scheduled medications and place John on comfort care in addition to his DNR/DNI code status.

After the care conference, the nurse discontinues all intravenous drips and John is transferred to the medical floor where he will be allowed to die.

What data from the current concern is important & RELEVANT; therefore it has clinical significance to the nurse?

RELEVANT Data from Current Concern:	Clinical Significance:
After Steve's angry outburst, the nurse communicates to the primary provider that a care conference needs to be scheduled as soon as possible. Two days later the care conference took place and all of John's family was in attendance as well as the medical treatment team.	*This is an example of how an engaged nurse can make a difference! If the nurse had taken Steve's anger personally, he/she would be inclined to disengage and not authentically care. Taking initiative to get all family together at the same time to dialogue in this setting is needed.*
The grim prognosis of his current status was presented and all questions were answered by the treatment team. Steve, the oldest son, asks numerous questions. John continues to insist that he wants all treatments stopped and just wants to die. After the care conference, there is a consensus between the family and treatment team to stop all supportive therapies including intravenous drips, most scheduled medications and place him on comfort care in addition to his DNR/DNI code status.	*This outcome can be attributed to facilitating this discussion SOONER and not later!* *Steve needed more time and answers than others in the family, but the strength of this family is that they were able to reach consensus and be at peace in a difficult and painful situation.* *It is a beautiful thing when a family can reach consensus and have peace of mind about these difficult decisions. When one member of the family suffers, they all do. This family has come to grips with the end of his life and to comfort and care for John and one another.*
After the care conference, the nurse discontinues all intravenous drips and John is transferred to the medical floor where he will be allowed to die.	*Though it is difficult to discontinue these medications knowing the ultimate outcome it will bring, the nurse can be at peace knowing that he/she advocated and honored the wishes of the patient.*

III. Resolving the Dilemma

1. Identifying data that is RELEVANT, what is the essence of this current dilemma?
John wants all treatments stopped and is opting for comfort care. This is John's decision and the nurse needs to advocate and support the family to make this possible.

There are essentially three goals of care for all patients:
- *Cure*
- *Stabilize*
- *Comfort*

John's condition has changed. For two weeks he was stabilized, but with his condition has deteriorated. John's plan has changed to the final goal, which is comfort care.

2. What additional information is needed by the nurse that would help clarify the current dilemma?
- *Is there a written living will that can be provided by the family?*
- *Where does the family draw its meaning and strength?*
- *What is the meaning of the end of this life to them spiritually? How does John process this spiritually?*
- *Where does Steve live? Was he just flying in from out of town? Or has he seen his father recently?*
- *Is there a pastor or a spiritual leader you can contact for them?*
- *What does this family envision as "comfort"?*

3. What additional members of the healthcare team could be used in this situation? Why?
- *Social worker. Depending on how long John lives after his status changes to comfort care, social workers are needed to coordinate home hospice.*
- *Pastoral care. Caring for the spirit is always relevant when dealing with death and dying. Make it a priority to address and allow the patient the option to decide what he may want whether he has a church affiliation or not.*
- *Nurse case manager. May need to help cooridinate with social services depending on the size of the hospital. Patient may become ready for hospice and this might be introduced. It may involve transfer to home or another facility.*

4. What is the nursing priority?
- *Treat the patient and the family. The family is central to John's care at this time in his life. In hospice, the patient and the family are considered one unit of care. Hospice is a big decision and this family will be considering the options in the next few days.*

- *Comfort. Comfort is NOT a NANDA nursing diagnostic statement, but what it represents may be. This includes symptom management, pain control, dyspnea management, and comfort for the family. Dyspnea management is an emphasis in oncology nursing and hospice and is relevant for John. Nursing interventions that address this include a fan on his face and morphine. Sometimes morphine nebs are used to administer it directly to the lungs without systemic effects.*

- *Death with dignity. Nurses need to do it right by showing authentic caring in their actions. Families will never forget what was done at the end of life.*

5. What nursing interventions and/or principles can the nurse use to successfully resolve this clinical dilemma?

- *Decrease fluid intake. Over-hydration increases the struggle with breathing, death rattle, edema, etc.*
- *What would comfort the patient? Ask the patient what he would like...Music, back rub, (use of touch can be very personal and some may not desire it), scripture to be read, or prayer.*
- *Teach family to moisten the mouth when the patient is unconscious and mouth breathing*
- *Patients can hear until the very end of life. Encourage the family to talk to the patient even when he can't respond.*
- *The nurse needs to advocate for the patient and his wishes. Hospice care is an excellent example of holistic nursing care that involves much more than ensuring adequate pain control with medications.*

This patient is requesting a new level of care called AND (Allow Natural Death). Conversations in the literature began in 2008 surrounding this terminology. It can be defined as "good end of life care should focus on what we as nurses provide than what we forgo" (American Nurses Association, 2012). Allowing a natural death simply means not interfering with the natural dying process while providing care to keep the patient as comfortable as possible. Simply said, it allows nature to take its course. At times it is difficult for health care professionals to allow this process to happen because they may feel that they have failed in some way. But in reality we have succeeded when one recognizes that death is a part of life that we will all face. Treat your patients as you would want to be treated in this context.

The Association of Perioperative Registered Nurses supports a reconsideration of DNR or allow-natural-death (AND) orders before surgical procedures and that all risks and benefits associated with surgery and anesthesia be discussed with patients who have DNR or AND orders in place before undergoing surgery (AORN, 2010). An order to allow natural death is meant to ensure that only comfort measures are provided. By using the AND, physicians and other medical professionals acknowledge that the patient is dying and that everything being done for the patient—including the withdrawal of nutrition and hydration—allows the dying process to occur as comfortably as possible."

The American Nurses Association recommends that:
1) Clinical nurses actively participate in timely and frequent discussions on changing goals of care and initiate DNR/AND discussions with patients and their families and
significant others.
2) Clinical nurses ensure that DNR orders are clearly documented, reviewed, and
updated periodically to reflect changes in the patient's condition (Joint Commission,
2010).
3) Nurse administrators ensure support for the clinical nurse to initiate DNR discussions

From ANA position paper written March 12, 2012 by ANA Center for Ethics and Human Rights.
http://www.nursingworld.org/MainMenuCategories/EthicsStandards/Ethics-Position-Statements/Nursing-Care-and-Do-Not-Resuscitate-DNR-and-Allow-Natural-Death-Decisions.pdf

6. What is the expected response of the patient that indicate the nursing interventions were effective?
The patient demonstrates one or more of the following:
- *Calm*
- *Pain is controlled*
- *Dyspnea controlled*
- *No death rattle*
- *Decreased urine output*
- *Family connected and remains on the same page*
- *Spiritual needs are met*

7. What response by the patient would indicate that a change in the plan of care and nursing interventions are needed?
The patient demonstrates one or more of the following:
- *Anxious*
- *Restless*
- *Dyspnea*
- *Audible death rattle*

8. What is the patient and/or family likely experiencing/feeling right now in this situation?
The family is experiencing numerous losses that all relate to grief and loss that must not be underestimated or minimized:
- *Loss of a loved one*
- *52 years of marriage and the loss of a best friend*
- *Father*
- *Fear of fully letting go and accepting of this outcome*

9. What can I do to engage myself with this patient's experience, and show that he/she matters to me as a person?
The following are some simple interventions that the nurse can do to engage and practically demonstrate caring:
- ***Go in the room regularly.*** *Though caring can feel awkward at times in this sacred moment avoid the temptation to stay out of the way and take the easy way out. Be willing to put yourself out there and be present as well as vulnerable.*
- ***Be present in the moment with them.*** *These first two interventions are closely related. There is no substitute for the caring presence of an engaged nurse. In this context nursing can make a difference that will be remembered forever by the family.*
- ***Offer comfort measures.*** *Be willing to offer food or beverages for this purpose. "Comfort food" is appropriate and should be included in any family comfort measures.*
- ***Teach family to do comfort measures*** *by helping them take initiative in caring for John by lubricating lips with Vaseline or swabbing mouth as needed to keep moist.*

- ***Talk to their loved one*** *even though he can't respond.*
- ***Converse and communicate with the family****. Small talk and anything that demonstrates that their needs matter and are important will build a bridge of support.*

10. What was learned from this case study that you will incorporate into your practice?
Content knowledge without personal application will not be fruitful. Reflection is an essential professional behavior that can also be practiced! I have added this question to allow students to intentionally reflect on what they have learned so that they can integrate this essential content into their practice and fully develop the ethical comportment of the professional nurse. This question will facilitate rich dialogue in whatever context you choose to use this case study. If there is not enough time to discuss this question, consider having students write a one-page reflection paper.

ETHICAL Dilemma

Medical Futility

STUDENT Worksheet

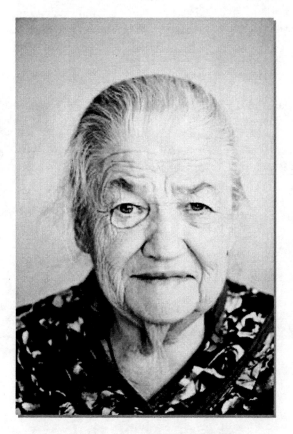

Mavis Anderson, 84 years old

Overview

This scenario highlights the ethical dilemma of medical futility when Mavis remains in ICU on a ventilator as a result of respiratory failure. She also has dementia and terminal cancer. The family is unwilling to consider withdrawing life support and one of the members is openly antagonistic and is not afraid to question and confront nurses about what he thinks is best for his mother.

Clinical Dilemma Activity: STUDENT

Medical Futility

I. Scenario

History of Present Problem:

Mavis Anderson is a frail, 84-year-old woman who was admitted to your medical unit six days ago after falling at home. She has a large hematoma on her right lateral hip. She is on warfarin daily for chronic atrial fibrillation. She has a history of stage IV breast cancer with metastasis to the liver, dementia, and COPD. Despite having only months to live, she is currently a full code. Mavis does not have a living will, but according to her son, who has the power of attorney (POA), she would want to live and wants everything done to support her.

Ten days ago Mavis developed progressive SOB with respiratory failure that required intubation and mechanical ventilation. CXR confirmed bilateral infiltrates consistent with aspiration pneumonia. She continues to require ventilator support with vent settings of AC: 12, TV: 500, PEEP: +5, FiO2: 60%. Bipap weans have lasted only 15 minutes before she becomes tachypneic with RR >30 and O2 sat that drops to <90%.

Personal/Social History:

Mavis lives in a skilled long-term care facility and is widowed. She has six children who are actively involved in her care and live in the area. The oldest son, Tom, is POA.

What data from the histories is important & RELEVANT; therefore it has clinical significance to the nurse?

RELEVANT Data from Present Problem:	Clinical Significance:

RELEVANT Data from Social History:	Clinical Significance:

II. The Dilemma Begins…

Current Concern:

Palliative care was consulted and the physician documented the following:

- Mavis is critically and terminally ill with no chance of recovery to return to her prior living arrangement. She would require ventilatory support at a long term-care-acute-care (LTAC) facility with 24/7 nursing care. Despite this assessment, the son Tom who is POA continues to insist that full ICU support be continued that includes ventilator, vasopressors (neosynephrine), and parenteral tube feedings.
- Mavis and her family are Catholic, and have faith and hope for a miraculous recovery which cannot happen unless Mavis is maximally supported in ICU. The son believes that removal of the ventilator support is akin to directly causing the death of his mother.
- Palliative Plan: Care conference with all family members, medical providers and nursing. The current grim prognosis and recommendations of medical team will be presented.

Tom is angry that his viewpoint does not seem to be considered by the medical providers. He openly shares his frustration and distrust of hospital staff including nursing. He has "fired" physicians who he does not feel are supportive of his wishes and current plan of care. He remains at his mother's bedside most of the day. He intently watches everything that is done, writes in a notebook as care is provided, and questions nurses in a confrontational tone of voice.

What data from the current concern is important & RELEVANT; therefore it has clinical significance to the nurse?

RELEVANT Data from Current Concern:	Clinical Significance:

III. Resolving the Dilemma

1. Identifying data that is RELEVANT, what is the essence of this current dilemma?

2. What additional information is needed by the nurse that would help clarify the current dilemma?

3. What additional members of the healthcare team could be used in this situation? Why?

4. What is the nursing priority?

5. What nursing interventions and/or principles can the nurse use to successfully resolve this clinical dilemma?

6. What is the expected response of the family that indicate the nursing interventions were effective?

7. What response by the family would indicate that a change in the plan of care and nursing interventions are needed?

8. What is the patient or family likely experiencing/feeling right now in this situation?

9. What can I do to engage myself with this patient's experience, and show that she matters to me as a person?

10. Does this scenario warrant a review by the medical ethics committee of the hospital? Why or why not?

11. What was learned from this case study that you will incorporate into your practice?

ETHICAL Dilemma
Medical Futility

Mavis Anderson, 84 years old

Answer Key

Clinical Dilemma Activity: ANSWER KEY

Medical Futility

I. Scenario

History of Present Problem:

Mavis Anderson is a frail, 84-year-old woman who was admitted to your medical unit six days ago after falling at home. She has a large hematoma on her right lateral hip. She is on warfarin daily for chronic atrial fibrillation. She has a history of stage IV breast cancer with metastasis to the liver, dementia, and COPD. Despite having only months to live, she is currently a full code. Mavis does not have a living will, but according to her son, who has the power of attorney (POA), she would want to live and wants everything done to support her.

Ten days ago Mavis developed progressive SOB with respiratory failure that required intubation and mechanical ventilation. CXR confirmed bilateral infiltrates consistent with aspiration pneumonia. She continues to require ventilator support with vent settings of AC: 12, TV: 500, PEEP: +5, FiO2: 60%. Bipap weans have lasted only 15 minutes before she becomes tachypneic with RR >30 and O2 sat that drops to <90%.

Personal/Social History:

Mavis lives in a skilled long-term care facility and is widowed. She has six children who are actively involved in her care and live in the area. The oldest son, Tom, is POA.

What data from the histories is important & RELEVANT; therefore it has clinical significance to the nurse?

RELEVANT Data from Present Problem:	Clinical Significance:
She has a history of stage IV breast cancer with metastasis to the liver, dementia, and COPD.	*This cluster of data makes it clear that Mavis is terminal. Depending on the progression and degree of metastasis, she has a limited amount of time to live. Because of her dementia, she most likely is dependent upon her family to make the best clinical judgments regarding her care.*
Despite having only months to live, she is currently a full code. Mavis does not have a living will, but according to her son who has the power of attorney (POA) she would want to live and wants everything done to support her.	*This confirms the degree of her terminal disease. Though her son has power of attorney, it is unclear what Mavis would have wanted under these circumstances and if she would want everything done. Though this can be assumed, that may not represent what she would have wanted.*
Ten days ago Mavis developed progressive SOB with respiratory failure that required intubation and mechanical ventilation.	*When this data is clustered with her COPD, this could be a potential problem that will not easily resolve or improve regardless of aggressive medical intervention due to her underlying lung disease.*
CXR confirmed bilateral infiltrates consistent with aspiration pneumonia.	*This data confirms the presence of pneumonia which can be treated with IV antibiotics, but in the context of intubation and COPD, the possibility exists that the patient may not be able to be weaned successfully from the ventilator.*
She continues to require ventilator support with vent settings of AC: 12, TV: 500, PEEP: +5, FiO2: 60%. Bipap weans of 5/5 have lasted only 15 minutes before she becomes tachypneic with RR >30 and O2 sat that drops to <90%.	*Though the vent settings are not clinically significant, if your nursing students are advanced, it would be good to review what these abbreviations mean and see if they remember their significance.* *What is important for the nurse to recognize is that the weans off of the ventilator lasting only 15 minutes before the clinical data of tachypnea and decreasing oxygenation confirm that Mavis is unable to tolerate this wean.* *It has been 10 days since she had the initial need for the ventilator. Any infectious process should have cleared by now. The inability to wean is an ominous finding that suggests that it is extremely unlikely that Mavis will ever be able to be weaned successfully off the ventilator.*

RELEVANT Data from Social History:	Clinical Significance:
Mavis lives in a skilled long-term care facility and is widowed.	*She is completely dependent on others for her care and has only her children to be her advocates.*
She has six children who are actively involved in her care and live in the area. The oldest son Tom is POA.	*With a large family it is important to note who has the legal authority to make decisions. In this scenario it is Tom.*

II. The Dilemma Begins...

Current Concern:

Palliative care was consulted and the physician documented the following:

- Mavis is critically and terminally ill with no chance of recovery to return to her prior living arrangement. She would require ventilatory support at a long term-care-acute-care (LTAC) facility with 24/7 nursing care. Despite this assessment, the son, Tom, who is POA, continues to insist that full ICU support be continued that includes ventilator, vasopressors (neosynephrine), and parenteral tube feedings.
- Mavis and her family are Catholic, and have faith and hope for a miraculous recovery which cannot happen unless Mavis is maximally supported in ICU. The son believes that removal of the ventilator support is akin to directly causing the death of his mother.
- Palliative Plan: Care conference with all family members, medical providers and nursing. The current grim prognosis and recommendations of the medical team will be presented.

Tom is angry that his viewpoint does not seem to be considered by the medical providers. He openly shares his frustration and distrust of hospital staff including nursing. He has "fired" physicians who he does not feel are supportive of his wishes and current plan of care. He remains at his mother's bedside most of the day. He intently watches everything that is done, writes in a notebook as care is provided, and questions nurses in a confrontational tone of voice.

What data from the current concern is important & RELEVANT; therefore it has clinical significance to the nurse?

RELEVANT Data from Current Concern:	Clinical Significance:
Mavis is critically and terminally ill with no chance of recovery to return to her prior living arrangement. She would require ventilatory support at a long term-care-acute-care (LTAC) facility with 24/7 nursing care.	*The conclusion that Mavis has no chance of recovery to her prior level of health and would require long-term ventilator support is significant. Unless there is literally divine intervention, Mavis will not be able to be weaned successfully off the ventilator. Though this in itself is a potential ethical dilemma for a patient with chronic health care problems such as dementia, when the patient is also terminally ill, this factor makes prolonging life in this context medically futile.*
Despite this assessment, the son, Tom, who is POA, continues to insist that full ICU support be continued that includes ventilator, vasopressors (neosynephrine), and parenteral tube feedings.	*Though the health care team would not likely support this aggressive level of care in a terminally ill patient, Tom, who is also POA, has the legal authority to authorize this treatment.*
Mavis and her family are Catholic, and have faith and hope for a miraculous recovery which cannot happen unless Mavis is maximally supported in ICU. The son believes that removal of the ventilator support is akin to directly causing the death of his mother.	*The faith of the family and belief in God must be supported by the nurse. The essence of spiritual care is to provide and offer hope even when there appears to be no hope. The Bible has numerous examples of Jesus healing the sick and even raising the dead. Other verses declare that, "For nothing will be impossible with God." Luke 1:37.* *It is important to give the family time to see for themselves the likely futility of ongoing care if Mavis does not improve. Remember that the early stage of grieving is DENIAL. Though there is evident tension in this scenario between the family and the care providers, it is the highest*

	priority for the nursing team to establish a strong relationship with the family, especially Tom, that is grounded in mutual care, respect, and trust. This trust relationship will make communication given by the nurses the ability to be heard and considered.
Tom is angry that his viewpoint does not seem to be considered by the medical providers. He openly shares his frustration and distrust of hospital staff including nursing.	*Whenever there is clear distrust from the family toward the medical team, this makes it a much higher priority to establish an authentic caring and trust relationship with Tom and the family. It is important that the nurse does NOT take sides, but provides opportunities to allow the family to share their feelings especially when they are not trusting of nurses.*
He has "fired" physicians who he does not feel are supportive of his wishes and current plan of care. He remains at his mother's bedside most of the day.	*Though a family member or patient has the ability to "fire" physicians and even nurses they may have a conflict with, this is not typical and is a RED FLAG that conflict with the family will not be easily resolved. Tom's decision to stay at the bedside is likely due to his lack of trust of the health care team.*
He intently watches everything that is done, writes in a notebook as care is provided, and questions nurses in a confrontational tone of voice.	*When family members are this intent on watching everything that is and write everything down as it takes place, it produces significant stress as the nurse attempts to provide care. Though it is easy to have an "us against them" attitude and place your own guard up and decline to authentically engage, I have found that it is most effective to defuse the high levels of stress by demonstrating care for the patient and understanding for the family and what they are going through in this time of crisis. An empathetic attitude is essential to remain engaged in both the patient's care and to provide care for the family.*

III. Resolving the Dilemma

1. Identifying data that is RELEVANT, what is the essence of this current dilemma?
There are essentially two dynamics operating in this scenario:

1. Medical futility. Is it in the best interest of the patient to provide aggressive and possibly painful medical interventions of life long ventilator support in someone who is terminally ill?

2. How to best handle the confrontational and adversarial approach that Tom the POA has toward the health care team.

2. What additional information is needed by the nurse that would help clarify the current dilemma?
Though one has no reason not to believe what the family has communicated regarding the desire that Mavis would want everything done to keep her alive, the presence of a living will signed by Mavis when she was legally competent would have been an effective and conclusive piece of information that could have clarified many potential ethical issues in this scenario.

Would Mavis have wanted everything done to keep her alive even if she required parenteral feedings and intubation/ventilator support? This document would have clarified this and respected the autonomy that Mavis had to make treatment decisions regardless of what the rest of the family may want.

3. What additional members of the healthcare team could be used in this situation? Why?
If a palliative care consult is available as it was in this scenario, this perspective provides needed clarification to determine the appropriate plan of medical care and if medical futility is an ethical concern. A chaplain would be an excellent choice to provide needed spiritual support, as well as share a different perspective from the scriptures that would support the Biblical viewpoint that, "For everything there is a season, and a time for every matter under heaven: a time to be born, and a time to die." Ecclesiastes 3:1-2.

Another Biblical viewpoint that this family may benefit from comes from the apostle Paul who wrote:

"O death, where is your victory?

O death, where is your sting? "The sting of death is sin, and the power of sin is the law. But thanks be to God, who gives us the victory through our Lord Jesus Christ." 1 Corinthians 15:55-57.

This passage and the entirety of the New Testament testify that because of the resurrection of Jesus Christ, there is the hope of eternal life.

Though it is natural for most patients and family to cling to physical life at all costs, for those with a faith background rooted in the Bible, this perspective provides a context to hold physical life on this earth loosely because of the assurance of heaven and eternal life in Christ.

If the nurse possesses this faith worldview and is comfortable sharing this with the family, it would be appropriate to share this with the family. Otherwise, the chaplain would be the best resource to support the family spiritually.

4. What is the nursing priority?
This is a unique scenario where there are actually two different sets of nursing priorities, one for the patient, Mavis, and one for the family, especially Tom.

Because Mavis is intubated and unresponsive, her nursing priority is physiologic and focused on oxygenation and the NANDA nursing diagnostic statement "Impaired gas exchange" captures the essence of her inability to wean off the ventilator.

The family needs are primarily psychosocial and include the following NANDA nursing diagnostic statements:
- *Ineffective coping*
- *Fear*
- *Grieving*
- *Powerlessness*
- *Stress overload*
- *Decisional conflict*

5. What nursing interventions and/or principles can the nurse use to successfully resolve this clinical dilemma?
Though the family has numerous psychosocial stressors that are reflected above, they all in essence have similar nursing interventions that have in common the need to provide care, support, and establish a trust relationship. This can be accomplished by:
- *Allowing the family to verbalize their concerns in a nonjudgmental attitude*
- *Remaining present and available to family*
- *Strive to be empathetic. Do NOT make assumptions about the family based on the experiences of other nurses or care providers. This is a nursing RED FLAG! As soon as a nurse makes an assumption, he/she is unable to truly care and be engaged.*
- *Provide chaplain support*
- *Social services consult may also be appropriate*

Consider the wellness-illness continuum
Wellness…………*…………Awareness of Illness ……………**………………death

Where are the expectations of each of the family members along this spectrum? (*)Tom seems to be aware that Mavis is ill, but anticipates she will be made well. (**)The medical team anticipates this illness will result in death. Other family members may be at different points along the spectrum. Therein lies the challenge to get everyone on the same page. It is best to "spread the burden" and get social work and the chaplain involved, along with the ethics committee.

6. What is the expected response of the family that indicate the nursing interventions were effective?
The goal/outcome for the family is to establish and build trust with the care team, including nursing. Improved trust by the family will become evident when Tom is less confrontational with nursing and care providers, is able to leave the bedside for periods of time, and does not write notes compulsively.

7. What response by the family would indicate that a change in the plan of care and nursing interventions are needed?
If an adversarial and confrontational tone remain evident with Tom and the manner that he relates to the health care team, this will need to be directly addressed in the context of a care conference with boundaries established that will respect the family as well as the care team.

8. What is the patient or family likely experiencing/feeling right now in this situation?
Because Mavis has dementia and is critically ill, it is difficult to know what she is specifically feeling in this situation. What can be more easily discerned are the needs of the family. It is obvious that Tom is experiencing powerlessness and is struggling to let go. It is essential for the nurse to remain empathetic, engaged, though it is extremely difficult because of the family dynamics that create additional stress and difficulty.

Regardless of the family dynamics, the nurse must maintain an attitude of respect and dignity for the humanity of Mavis. It is not uncommon for other nurses or care providers to make denigrating comments regarding those whose quality of life does not meet the standards that they would want to have for themselves. Nurses must recognize the inherent value and sanctity in every patient they care for regardless of their physiologic status. This is the essence of what made Mother Teresa such a recognized and respected figure. She showed the same dignity and respect to the dying poor in India who were not valued because of their low caste as she would have shown to someone of a higher social standing..

9. What can I do to engage myself with this patient's experience, and show that she matters to me as a person?
The essence of empathy is to put oneself in the shoes of those you are caring for or the family and how they are responding. If the nurse can consciously make this transition, it becomes much easier to be moved with a heart of compassion for those that one cares for.

Swanson (1991) identified the following caring interventions in the practice setting that have relevance in this scenario to engage with this patient's experience and support both the patient and family in this crisis:

Family caring interventions
- *Maintain a hope-filled attitude*
- *Offer realistic optimism*
- *Support the family*
- *Explain all that is taking place and answer any/all questions*
- *Convey availability to the family*

Patient caring interventions
- *Preserve the dignity of the patient*
- *Anticipate needs*
- *Comfort the patient in any way*
- *Seek cues by paying close attention to the patient's response and anticipate her expected response*
- *Perform competently and skillfully as a nurse. This communicates caring to your patient!*
- *Convey availability to the patient*

10. Does this scenario warrant a review by the medical ethics committee of the hospital? Why or why not?
Absolutely. It is important to note that the nurse or any member of the health care team can notify the medical ethics team whenever there is a concern of an ethical nature that makes the nurse uncomfortable. Some examples of potential triggers for an ethical team consult are derived from the policy of the organization where I currently practice:
- *Unresolved conflict about care-related decision-making for the patient.*
- *Failure to respect, or confusion about, a patient's written or verbal health care directive.*
- *A difference of opinion about a patient's capacity to make an informed decision.*
- *Questions concerning patient rights, treatment options, or informed consent.*
- *Confusion or disagreement about medical orders to limit intervention (e.g. DNR or Comfort Care orders).*
- *The patient's wishes are not known by the substitute-decision maker, and life-sustaining treatments or interventions may be withdrawn.*

• *Questions about patient or substitute decision-maker choices when the benefits and burdens of a particular treatment appear to be equal or when intervention may be seen as medically futile or harmful to the patient.(Clinical Ethics Consultation. n.d.).)*

11.What was learned from this case study that you will incorporate into your practice?
Content knowledge without personal application will not be fruitful. Reflection is an essential professional behavior that can also be practiced! I have added this question to allow students to intentionally reflect on what they have learned so that they can integrate this essential content into their practice and fully develop the ethical comportment of the professional nurse. This question will facilitate rich dialogue in whatever context you choose to use this case study. If there is not enough time to discuss this question, consider having students write a one-page reflection paper.

References

Clinical Ethics Consultation. Accessed from http://akn.allina.com/content1/groups/patient-care/@akn-qst/documents/policies_procedures/sys-pc-aec-003.pdf#search=%22ethics consult%22

Swanson, K. M. (1991). Empirical development of a middle range theory of caring. *Nursing Research, 40*(3), 161–166.

ETHICAL Dilemma

Code Status/Patient Autonomy

STUDENT Worksheet

Mabel Miller, 84 years old

Overview

This clinical dilemma highlights the current code status of Mabel who has severe dementia and was recently extubated. She expressed to her husband years ago that she would not want to be kept alive long-term on a ventilator. Because of end-stage COPD, her primary care providers have communicated that if she required intubation for any reason in the future, she would likely remain on a ventilator the rest of her life. Her husband has not yet taken the initiative to honor Mabel's stated wishes and she remains a full code.

Clinical Dilemma Activity: STUDENT

Code Status/Patient Autonomy

I. Scenario

History of Present Problem:
Mabel Miller is an 84-year-old woman with a history of senile dementia, COPD, and CVA with dysphagia requiring gastrostomy tube. She was admitted eighteen days ago to the ICU for respiratory failure due to COPD and influenza and was intubated and placed on mechanical ventilation. Mabel was successfully extubated after ten days on the ventilator and has been transferred to the medical floor where she is currently on oxygen per nasal cannula at 4 liters. Her husband has been told by the physician that if she needed to be reintubated, she would likely remain on a ventilator for the rest of her life.

Personal/Social History:
Mabel is unable to recognize any family members and is non-verbal. She resides in a skilled-care facility and would return to this setting after she is discharged. Jim, her husband of 58 years is active and involved in her cares at the hospital. He stays at the hospital and spends each night sleeping in a recliner in her room. He openly shows tenderness and kindness towards Mabel and asks appropriate questions of the nurse regarding her care.

What data from the histories is important & RELEVANT; therefore it has clinical significance to the nurse?

RELEVANT Data from Present Problem:	Clinical Significance:
RELEVANT Data from Social History:	Clinical Significance:

II. The Dilemma Begins...

Current Concern:
Since Mabel has been extubated, she remains a full code. Jim acknowledges that Mabel communicated to him many years ago that she would not want to be kept alive on a ventilator, but he has been reluctant to change her code status from full code to do not intubate (DNI) despite what the primary care providers have told him.

What data from the current concern is important & RELEVANT; therefore it has clinical significance to the nurse?

RELEVANT Data from Current Concern:	Clinical Significance:

© 2015 Keith Rischer/www.KeithRN.com

III. Resolving the Dilemma

1. Identifying data that is RELEVANT, what is the essence of this current dilemma?

2. What additional information is needed by the nurse that would help clarify the current dilemma?

3. What additional members of the healthcare team could be used in this situation? Why?

4. What is the nursing priority?

5. What nursing interventions and/or principles can the nurse use to successfully resolve this clinical dilemma?

6. What is the expected response of the husband that indicate the nursing interventions were effective?

7. What response by the husband would indicate that a change in the plan of care and nursing interventions are needed?

8. What is the patient or family likely experiencing/feeling right now in this situation?

9. What can I do to engage myself with this patient's experience, and show that she matters to me as a person?

10. Does this scenario warrant a review by the medical ethics committee of the hospital? Why or why not?

11. What was learned from this case study that you will incorporate into your practice?

ETHICAL Dilemma

Code Status/Patient Autonomy

Mabel Miller, 84 years old

Answer Key

Clinical Dilemma Activity: ANSWER KEY

Full Code and End-Stage Respiratory Failure

I. Scenario

History of Present Problem:

Mabel Miller is an 84-year-old woman with a history of senile dementia, COPD, and CVA with dysphagia requiring gastrostomy tube. She was admitted eighteen days ago to the ICU for respiratory failure due to COPD and influenza and was intubated and placed on mechanical ventilation. Mabel was successfully extubated after ten days on the ventilator and has been transferred to the medical floor where she is currently on oxygen per nasal cannula at 4 liters. Her husband has been told by the physician that if she needed to be reintubated, she would likely remain on a ventilator for the rest of her life.

Personal/Social History:

Mabel is unable to recognize any family members and is non-verbal. She resides in a skilled-care facility and would return to this setting after she is discharged. Jim, her husband of 58 years, is active and involved in her care at the hospital. He stays at the hospital and spends each night sleeping in a recliner in her room. He openly shows tenderness and kindness towards Mabel and asks appropriate questions of the nurse regarding her care.

What data from the histories is important & RELEVANT; therefore it has clinical significance to the nurse?

RELEVANT Data from Present Problem:	Clinical Significance:
She was admitted eighteen days ago to the ICU for respiratory failure due to COPD and influenza and was intubated and placed on mechanical ventilation.	*Though she is now on the medical floor, this cluster of data communicates that Mabel was critically ill with severe respiratory failure. The clinical relationship between COPD, influenza, and intubation must be seen as a series of pathophysiologic "dominos." Because of her COPD she became much more susceptible to developing influenza. Her already damaged and scarred lungs from COPD compromised her even further, requiring mechanical intubation.*
Mabel was successfully extubated after ten days on the ventilator and has been transferred to the medical floor where she is currently on oxygen per nasal cannula at 4 liters.	*Ten days on the ventilator is a long time! In ICU, if a patient is unable to be successfully weaned off the ventilator after 14 days, they are considered a candidate for a tracheostomy. Once her intubation time is noted, her current O2 needs of 4 liters per n/c make it evident that her current condition has significantly improved and suggests stability.*
Her husband has been told by the physician that if she needed to be reintubated, she would likely remain on a ventilator for the rest of her life.	*Life-long ventilator support is an obvious major life change that has direct implications to quality of life vs. quantity or length of life. Though this debate can be an ethical slippery slope, the overall medical history of the patient needs to be considered. Mabel has had a prior stroke as well as senile dementia. She is unable to recognize family members. Are Mabel's wishes known? Does she want to be kept alive via mechanical ventilation the rest of her life? The ethical principle of autonomy must be considered and explored to determine her code status.* *Though human life is sacred and has inherent value, use this scenario to engage in a lively ethical debate in your classroom where you serve as the moderator!*
RELEVANT Data from Social History:	Clinical Significance:
Mabel is unable to recognize any family members and is non-verbal. She resides in a skilled-care facility and would return to this setting after she is discharged.	*This information is relevant because it will help to determine discharge planning knowing that she does not live at home with her husband.*
Jim, her husband of 58 years is active and involved in her cares at the hospital. He stays	*Actions do speak louder than words! The response of her husband to Mabel's current condition demonstrates sacrificial love and caring. He*

at the hospital and spends each night sleeping in a recliner in her room. He openly shows tenderness and kindness towards Mabel and asks appropriate questions of the nurse regarding her care.	*remains deeply committed to Mabel despite her inability to recognize him. By asking appropriate questions related to his wife, he communicates care to the nurses and does so in a way that is not confrontational or demonstrates a lack of trust.*

II. The Dilemma Begins…

Current Concern:
Since Mabel has been extubated, she remains a full code. Jim acknowledges that Mabel communicated to him many years ago that she would not want to be kept alive on a ventilator, but he has been reluctant to change her code status from full code to do not intubate (DNI) despite what the primary care providers have told him.

What data from the current concern is important & RELEVANT; therefore it has clinical significance to the nurse?

RELEVANT Data from Current Concern:	Clinical Significance:
Since Mabel has been extubated, she remains a full code.	*This may or may not be an ethical dilemma depending on what Mabel expressed to her husband when she was competent and her wishes regarding end of life care.*
Jim acknowledges that Mabel communicated to him many years ago that she would not want to be kept alive on a ventilator, but he has been reluctant to change her code status from full code to do not intubate (DNI) despite what the primary care providers have told him.	*Now that this data is known, this is a potential ethical dilemma that needs to be addressed by the health care team. Though she is currently clinically stable, considering the severity of her earlier respiratory failure, her status could quickly change, if not in this hospitalization, then in the near future because she remains a susceptible host. Based on the interactions that the nurse has observed between Jim and Mabel, it is likely that Jim is having a hard time letting go and making a decision that has life-long implications.*

III. Resolving the Dilemma

1. Identifying data that is RELEVANT, what is the essence of this current dilemma?
Respecting the autonomy of Mabel who has communicated to her husband that she would NOT want to be kept alive on a ventilator, and the need to support her husband as he considers making her a DNI code status despite what he may want.

2. What additional information is needed by the nurse that would help clarify the current dilemma?
Though the husband has communicated that Mabel would not want to remain intubated long-term, it is important for the nurse to ask if there is a living will that Mabel made while she was competent that would clarify her intent and wishes regarding end-of-life care.

It would also be beneficial to determine if Jim and/or Mabel have a faith tradition that is an important part of their life. Choices made at end of life often have spiritual dimensions and considerations that must be addressed. This is not known at this time, but is important information that the nurse should gather.

3. What additional members of the healthcare team could be used in this situation? Why?
In addition to engaging the primary care provider to have a direct discussion on code status with Jim, another resource the nurse may want to consider is a chaplain, depending on the response the nurse obtains from question #2.

4. What is the nursing priority?
This is a unique scenario. There are actually two different sets of nursing priorities, one for the patient, Mabel, and one for her husband, Jim.
Because Mabel remains on O2, her nursing priority remains physiologic and focused on oxygenation. The NANDA nursing diagnostic statement "Impaired gas exchange" captures the essence of her current status.
Her husband's needs are primarily psychosocial and could include the following NANDA nursing diagnostic statements:
- *Grieving*
- *Decisional conflict*

5. What nursing interventions and/or principles can the nurse use to successfully resolve this clinical dilemma?
Jim requires emotional support from the nurse to help clarify his desires and what his wife would want regarding code status. Jim may be having difficulty saying goodbye and losing his lifelong friend and companion. This assumption needs to be clarified so that the expressed wishes of Mabel are honored.
- *Allow Jim to verbalize any concerns in a nonjudgmental attitude*
- *Remain present and available to Jim*
- *Strive to be empathetic and do NOT make assumptions about this dilemma based on the experiences of other nurses or care providers. This is a nursing RED FLAG! As soon as a nurse makes an assumption, he/she is unable to truly care and be engaged.*
- *Provide chaplain support for Jim if this is something that he would want or value.*

6. What is the expected response of the husband that indicate the nursing interventions were effective?
The goal would be for Jim to be able to openly share his feelings and any struggle he may have regarding his perspective in continuing to leave Mabel in a full code status. If a specific nurse has established a therapeutic relationship, this dialogue could take place between the husband and nursing or primary care provider, social services, or chaplaincy.

7. What response by the husband would indicate that a change in the plan of care and nursing interventions are needed?
If the husband would not verbalize his feelings regarding code status or remains adamant about continuing a full code status despite the stated wishes of his wife, this is a concern that could warrant a review by the facility's medical ethics committee..

8. What is the patient and/or family likely experiencing/feeling right now in this situation?
Because Mabel has senile dementia and is nonverbal, it is difficult to know what she is specifically feeling in this situation. What can be more easily discerned are the needs of the family, specifically her husband. It is obvious that he is conflicted and struggling to let go. It is essential for the nurse to remain empathetic, engaged, and maintain an attitude of respect and dignity for the humanity of Mabel, though she has such limited cognitive function. It is not uncommon for other nurses or care providers to make denigrating comments regarding those whose quality of life does not meet the standards that they would want to have for themselves.
I strongly encourage nurses to see the inherent value and sanctity in every patient they care for regardless of their physiologic status. This is the essence of what made Mother Teresa such a recognized and respected figure. She showed the same dignity and respect to the dying poor in India who were not valued because of their low caste as she did people of a high socioeconomic status.

9. What can I do to engage myself with this patient's experience, and show that she matters to me as a person?
The essence of empathy is to put oneself in the shoes of those you are caring for or the family and monitor their response. If the nurse can consciously make this transition, it becomes much easier to be moved with a heart of compassion for those that one cares for.

Swanson (1991) the following caring interventions in the practice setting that have relevance in this scenario to engage with this patient's experience and support both the patient and family in this crisis:

Family caring interventions
- *Maintain a hope-filled attitude*
- *Offer realistic optimism*
- *Support the family*
- *Explain all that is taking place and answer any/all questions*
- *Convey availability to the family*

Patient caring interventions
- *Preserve the dignity of the patient*
- *Anticipate needs*
- *Comfort the patient in any way*
- *Seek cues by paying close attention to the patient's response and anticipate her expected response*

- *Perform competently and skillfully as a nurse. This communicates caring to your patient!*
- *Convey availability to the patient*

10.Does this scenario warrant a review by the medical ethics committee of the hospital? Why or why not?

Some examples of potential triggers for an ethical team consult are derived from the policy of the organization where I currently practice clinically:
- *Unresolved conflict about care-related decision-making for the patient.*
- *Failure to respect, or confusion about, a patient's written or verbal health care directive.*
- *A difference of opinion about a patient's capacity to make an informed decision.*
- *Questions concerning patient rights, treatment options, or informed consent.*
- *Confusion or disagreement about medical orders to limit intervention (e.g. DNR or Comfort Care orders).*
- *The patient's wishes are not known by the substitute-decision maker, and life-sustaining treatments or interventions may be withdrawn.*
- *Questions about patient or substitute decision-maker choices when the benefits and burdens of a particular treatment appear to be equal or when intervention may be seen as medically futile or harmful to the patient.(1)*

IF the husband insisted on maintaining a full code status despite the stated wishes of his wife, this could meet the criteria to have an ethics consult based upon the first criteria, "Unresolved conflict about care-related decision-making for the patient."

11.What was learned from this case study that you will incorporate into your practice?

Content knowledge without personal application will not be fruitful. Reflection is an essential professional behavior that can also be practiced! I have added this question to allow students to intentionally reflect on what they have learned so that they can integrate this essential content into their practice and fully develop the ethical comportment of the professional nurse. This question will facilitate rich dialogue in whatever context you choose to use this case study. If there is not enough time to discuss this question, consider having students write a one-page reflection paper.

References

Clinical Ethics Consultation. Accessed from http://akn.allina.com/content1/groups/patient-care/@akn-qst/documents/policies_procedures/sys-pc-aec-003.pdf#search=%22ethics consult%22

Swanson, K. M. (1991). Empirical development of a middle range theory of caring. *Nursing Research, 40*(3), 161–166.

ETHICAL Dilemma

Remain Intubated or Withdraw Life Support

STUDENT Worksheet

Joyce Johnson, 58 years old

Overview

When a patient has a stroke, is intubated, and unable to wean off the ventilator, what can be done to ensure the patient's autonomy when there is no living will and no family that can be contacted to guide this decision-making process of a vulnerable adult?

Clinical Dilemma Activity: STUDENT
Remain Intubated or Withdraw Life Support
I. Scenario
History of Present Problem:
Joyce Johnson is a 58-year-old woman with a history of atrial fibrillation, COPD, and depression. A friend who had not heard from her for two days became concerned and went to her home. She found Joyce unresponsive on the floor of her living room. She had a large left middle cerebral artery (MCA) ischemic stroke. She is intubated and has remained in ICU since she was admitted to the hospital five days ago. She is also in acute renal failure as a result of rhabdomyolosis and requires daily dialysis.

Personal/Social History:
Joyce is divorced, and has one adult daughter. She is estranged from her siblings and has not spoken to her daughter in five years. She is on disability for severe depression. Depending on how she feels, Joyce inconsistently takes scheduled medications including warfarin.

What data from the histories is important & RELEVANT; therefore it has clinical significance to the nurse?

RELEVANT Data from Present Problem:	Clinical Significance:

RELEVANT Data from Social History:	Clinical Significance:

II. The Dilemma Begins...
Current Concern:
Ten days after her CVA, Joyce remains on the ventilator and has failed repeated attempts to wean from the ventilator. She no longer requires dialysis. She does not have a living will and her wishes for treatment are unknown. A care conference is planned as soon as possible. Social services has been unable to contact her ex-husband or daughter.

What data from the current concern is important & RELEVANT; therefore it has clinical significance to the nurse?

RELEVANT Data from Current Concern:	Clinical Significance:

III. Resolving the Dilemma

1. *Identifying data that is RELEVANT, what is the essence of this current dilemma?*

2. *What additional information is needed by the nurse that would help clarify the current dilemma?*

3. *What additional members of the healthcare team could be used in this situation? Why?*

4. *What is the nursing priority?*

5. *What nursing interventions and/or principles can the nurse use to successfully resolve this clinical dilemma?*

6. *What is the patient likely experiencing/feeling right now in this situation?*

7. *What can I do to engage myself with this patient's experience, and show that she matters to me as a person?*

8. *Does this scenario warrant a review by the medical ethics committee of the hospital? Why or why not?*

9. *What was learned from this case study that you will incorporate into your practice?*

ETHICAL Dilemma

Remain Intubated or Withdraw Life Support

Joyce Johnson, 58 years old

Answer Key

Clinical Dilemma Activity: ANSWER KEY
Remain Intubated or Withdraw Life Support
I. Scenario
History of Present Problem:
Joyce Johnson is a 58-year-old woman with a history of atrial fibrillation, COPD, and depression. A friend who had not heard from her for two days became concerned and went to her home. She found Joyce unresponsive on the floor of her living room. She had a large left middle cerebral artery (MCA) ischemic stroke. She is intubated and has remained in ICU since she was admitted to the hospital five days ago. She is also in acute renal failure as a result of rhabdomyolosis and requires daily dialysis.

Personal/Social History:
Joyce is divorced, and has one adult daughter. She is estranged from her siblings and has not spoken to her daughter in five years. She is on disability for severe depression. Depending on how she feels, Joyce inconsistently takes scheduled medications including warfarin.

What data from the histories is important & RELEVANT; therefore it has clinical significance to the nurse?

RELEVANT Data from Present Problem:	Clinical Significance:
She was found on the floor of her living room unresponsive. She had a large left middle cerebral artery (MCA) ischemic stroke.	*Why would a relatively young woman experience an ischemic stroke? There is a clinical relationship that must be identified by the nurse regarding her history of atrial fibrillation and the ischemic stroke. This is one of the most common complications of atrial fibrillation and is why warfarin or other anticoagulants are taken daily by those patients.*
She is intubated and has remained in ICU since she was admitted to the hospital five days ago.	*Joyce is critically ill and remains intubated. This is an ominous sign, though it is too early to determine if she will be a long-term ventilated patient.*
She is also in acute renal failure as a result of rhabdomyolosis and requires daily dialysis.	*Why would Joyce develop acute renal failure as a result of rhabdomyolysis? What in her history could be the cause? Unfortunately, this is a common complication when a patient is found down and has been immobile for at least 12 to 24 hours. Because of a lack of movement and lying in one place, muscle begins to break down. As a result, the proteins of this breakdown impact glomerular function and result in kidney failure. This clinical relationship is important for the nurse to identify and recognize that rhabdomyolosis did not happen as a result of her stroke.*
RELEVANT Data from Social History:	**Clinical Significance:**
Joyce is divorced, and has one adult daughter. She is estranged from her siblings and has not spoken to her daughter in five years.	*This is a psychosocial red flag and clinical concern! Though most patients have some psychosocial and family support, Joyce does not. This could be a potential problem as it relates to treatment decisions regarding her future care.*
She is on disability for severe depression. Depending on how she feels, Joyce inconsistently takes scheduled medications including warfarin.	*Though an ischemic stroke can still happen when a patient is on warfarin and properly anticoagulated, it is much more difficult. Unfortunately, Joyce has not been consistently compliant in taking her warfarin and as a result this was likely the reason she experienced an embolic stroke. This is also an excellent example of how psychiatric and emotional states of mind can directly impact the body.*

II. The Dilemma Begins…

Current Concern:
Ten days after her CVA, Joyce remains on the ventilator and has failed repeated attempts to wean from the ventilator. She no longer requires dialysis. She does not have a living will and her wishes for treatment are unknown. A care conference is planned as soon as possible. Social services has been unable to contact her ex-husband or daughter.

What data from the current concern is important & RELEVANT; therefore it has clinical significance to the nurse?

RELEVANT Data from Current Concern:	Clinical Significance:
Ten days after her CVA, Joyce remains on the ventilator and has failed repeated attempts to wean from the ventilator. She no longer requires dialysis.	*This is an ominous sign. An inability to wean off the ventilator will likely require a tracheostomy and ventilator for long-term support. The only silver lining is that she will not require ongoing dialysis as a result of her rhabdomyolysis and her initial presentation of acute renal failure.*
She does not have a living will and her wishes for treatment are unknown.	*Though it is not uncommon for middle-aged adults to not have a living will, knowing and honoring Joyce's wishes in this situation will be very difficult. The ethical principle of autonomy is good, but the wishes of the individual must first be known in order for this principle to be honored.*
A care conference is planned as soon as possible. Social services has been unable to contact her ex-husband or daughter.	*Though a care conference is obviously needed, it is extremely concerning that there will likely be no family to directly communicate what Joyce would have wanted under these circumstances.*

III. Resolving the Dilemma

1. Identifying data that is RELEVANT, what is the essence of this current dilemma?
Joyce will likely require lifelong ventilatory support with a tracheostomy. It is unknown what her wishes would be regarding this level of ongoing care. How can autonomy of the patient can be honored if it is not known is the essence of this clinical dilemma.

2. What additional information is needed by the nurse that would help clarify the current dilemma?
To identify the wishes of the patient if they have been expressed verbally to family or even friends. Ideally this information would be most relevant if it came from direct family. But if they cannot be found, then using any information that a friend could provide would be needed and relevant. Because this person can be identified, she must attend and be a part of the care conference to help guide the decision-making process of the treatment team.

Another important piece of information that is not clearly known at this time is Joyce's cognitive function. Has an EEG been done, and if so, what were the results? This will have a strong influence regarding the decision to continue ventilatory support or to withdraw.

3. What additional members of the healthcare team could be used in this situation? Why?
Social services is the most important additional member of the treatment team in this case.. Using their investigative ability to help identify and track down family members and coordinate appropriate discharge planning is essential.

4. What is the nursing priority?
There is no NANDA nursing diagnostic statement that fits this scenario as a nursing priority. From my perspective, the nurse must embrace the role of patient advocate when there is no one to speak up or be a voice. Though medical ethics can get fuzzy with quality of life versus sanctity of life, it is imperative that the nurse errs on the side of life and advocate for this perspective, even if the treatment team may want to consider withdrawing ventilatory support. The nurse must remain true to an internal compass that has a high regard for the value for all human life, even those who have severe or permanent disabilities.
Though some may disagree with this perspective, use this thought to engage and create a rich ethical discussion in your classroom!

5. What nursing interventions and/or principles can the nurse use to successfully resolve this clinical dilemma?
I would emphasize the importance of nurse advocacy as an essential nursing intervention as well as the principle of the value and sanctity of human life. Though culture and many medical ethicists tend to see human life that does not have a certain degree of cognitive functioning as something less than human, I believe it is important that nursing remains true to our core ethic to demonstrate and show compassion to those who are vulnerable, defenseless and unable to advocate for themselves.

What gives human life its inherent value and worth?
As one who embraces a Biblical worldview, Genesis 1 makes it very clear that not only did God create all things, but that human life is unique and distinctly created in His image. Though this worldview may not be as dominant as it once was, I believe that it remains true. As the nurse who is caring for Joyce, it is important to appropriately take a stand and share this in the context of any care conference or medical ethics consult that may take place regarding the issues that this dilemma represents.

6. What is the patient likely experiencing/feeling right now in this situation?
Because we do not know Joyce's mental status and cognitive capabilities, this is difficult to state conclusively. Regardless of the cognitive functioning of this patient, it is essential for the nurse to continue to treat her with dignity and respect in all interactions.

7. What can I do to engage myself with this patient's experience, and show that she matters to me as a person?
Though the patient may be unresponsive, I have found one simple way to demonstrate caring and treat a patient such as Joyce with dignity and respect is to communicate verbally everything I am going to do before I do it. I assume that she understands even though she may not. I also make it a priority to have her physical appearance as presentable as possible such as having her hair combed, etc. In nursing, the little things that are done are really the BIG things that can make a significant difference!

The essence of empathy is to put oneself in the shoes of those you are caring for or the family and how they are responding. If the nurse can consciously make this transition, it becomes much easier to be moved with a heart of compassion for those that one cares for.

Swanson (1991) the following caring interventions in the practice setting that have relevance in this scenario to support the patient in this crisis:
Patient caring interventions
- *Preserve the dignity of the patient*
- *Comfort the patient in any way*
- *Seek cues by paying close attention to the patient's response and anticipate her expected response*
- *Perform competently and skillfully as a nurse. This communicates caring to your patient!*

8. Does this scenario warrant a review by the medical ethics committee of the hospital? Why or why not?
Absolutely!
In fact, it is imperative that the nurse is proactive and even initiates this consult early on because of the significant issues that it raises based on what we know.

It is important to note that the nurse or any member of the health care team can notify the medical ethics team whenever there is a concern of an ethical nature that the nurse is not comfortable with. Some examples of potential triggers for an ethical team consult are derived from the policy of the organization where I currently practice :
- *Unresolved conflict about care-related decision-making for the patient.*
- *Failure to respect, or confusion about, a patient's written or verbal health care directive.*
- *A difference of opinion about a patient's capacity to make an informed decision.*
- *Questions concerning patient rights, treatment options, or informed consent.*
- *Confusion or disagreement about medical orders to limit intervention (e.g. DNR or Comfort Care orders).*
- *The patient's wishes are not known by the substitute-decision maker, and life sustaining treatments or interventions may be withdrawn.*

• Questions about patient or substitute decision-maker choices when the benefits and burdens of a particular treatment appear to be equal or when intervention may be seen as medically futile or harmful to the patient (Clinical Ethics Consultation, n.d.).

9. What was learned from this case study that you will incorporate into your practice?
Content knowledge without personal application will not be fruitful. Reflection is an essential professional behavior that can also be practiced! I have added this question to allow students to intentionally reflect on what they have learned so that they can integrate this essential content into their practice and fully develop the ethical comportment of the professional nurse. This question will facilitate rich dialogue in whatever context you choose to use this case study. If there is not enough time to discuss this question, consider having students turn this in as a separate one page reflection paper.

References

Clinical Ethics Consultation. Accessed from http://akn.allina.com/content1/groups/patient-care/@akn-qst/documents/policies_procedures/sys-pc-aec-003.pdf#search=%22ethics consult%22

Swanson, K. M. (1991). Empirical development of a middle range theory of caring. *Nursing Research, 40*(3), 161–166.

NURSE Dilemma

Nurse to Student Incivility

STUDENT Worksheet

Cindy Benner, 21 years old

Overview

Incivility is endemic in nursing. This dilemma identifies the most common uncivil behaviors that students may experience from nurses in the clinical setting and how to respectfully address this if experienced. This activity will empower students to be the needed change so a culture of civility that honors and respects the differences of others can be realized in the nursing profession.

Clinical Dilemma Activity: STUDENT

Nurse to Student Incivility

I. Scenario

History of Present Problem:

Cindy Benner is a 21-year-old nursing student who is in the third year of her baccalaureate program at a local state university. She is an excellent student and is excited to pursue her dream and passion to become a professional nurse. She has enjoyed clinical learning and is excited to begin a new rotation on the medical unit at a local hospital. She has completed pre-clinical prep and introduces herself to Jennifer, the primary nurse of her patient. Jennifer looks at her and rolls her eyes. She gives a quick report to Cindy, does not maintain eye contact, and promptly hurries down the hall, stating she has to get to work or she will get behind.

What data from the histories is important & RELEVANT; therefore it has clinical significance to the nurse?

RELEVANT Data from Present Problem:	Clinical Significance:

II. The Dilemma Begins…

Current Concern:

Cindy completes her initial assessment of her patient, a 68 year-old woman who presented to the hospital with a ruptured appendix and is now post-operative day one. Her temperature has increased to 101.2 (last recorded was 99.5), her heart rate is 98 (last recorded was 76) and her blood pressure is 98/60 (last recorded was 120/66). Cindy just had a classroom lecture on sepsis and the inflammatory response. Though an inflammatory response is expected after surgery, the instructor emphasized that systemic inflammatory response syndrome (SIRS) is an early predicator for sepsis that could progress to septic shock. SIRS criteria include temperature >100.4, heart rate >90 and decreasing blood pressure.

Cindy approaches Jennifer to share her concern that her patient may be developing sepsis. Jennifer appears irritated, and states in an angry tone, "I was just in her room an hour ago and she looked just fine. I think you are overreacting. I've been a nurse for twenty years. Do you think a student knows more than me? I don't think so! I will check on her when I get a chance."

What data from the current concern is important & RELEVANT; therefore it has clinical significance to the nurse?

RELEVANT Data from Current Concern:	Clinical Significance:

© 2015 Keith Rischer/www.KeithRN.com

III. Resolving the Dilemma

1. *Identifying data that is RELEVANT, what is the essence of this current dilemma?*

2. *What additional information is needed by the student that would help clarify the current dilemma?*

3. *What additional members of the healthcare team could be utilized in this situation? Why?*

4. *What is the priority?*

5. *What interventions and/or principles can be used by the student to successfully resolve this clinical dilemma?*

6. *What is the expected response that would indicate interventions were effective?*

7. *What is the student likely experiencing/feeling right now in this situation?*

8. *What are the uncivil behaviors demonstrated by the staff nurse in this situation?*

9. *Have you personally experienced uncivil or bullying behaviors? If so, how did it make you feel?*

10. *What have you learned from this case study that you will incorporate into your practice?*

NURSE Dilemma

Nurse to Student Incivility

Cindy Benner, 21 years old

Answer Key

Clinical Dilemma Activity: ANSWER KEY
Nurse to Student Incivility
I. Scenario
History of Present Problem:
Cindy Benner is a 21-year-old nursing student who is in the third year of her baccalaureate program at a local state university. She is an excellent student and is excited to pursue her dream and passion to become a professional nurse. She has enjoyed clinical learning and is excited to begin a new rotation on the medical unit at a local hospital. She has completed pre-clinical prep and introduces herself to Jennifer, the primary nurse of her patient. Jennifer looks at her and rolls her eyes. She gives a quick report to Cindy, does not maintain eye contact, and promptly hurries down the hall, stating she has to get to work or she will get behind.

What data from the histories is important & RELEVANT; therefore it has clinical significance to the nurse?

RELEVANT Data from Present Problem:	Clinical Significance:
She is an excellent student and is excited to pursue her dream and passion to become a professional nurse.	*Though this information may not seem at first glance relevant, in the context of incivility, it is. When incivility is experienced personally, it wounds deeply and has the power to destroy the joy and purpose that a student or even a nurse in practice has to continue to be a caregiver.*
She has completed pre-clinical prep and introduces herself to Jennifer, her nursing partner. Jennifer looks at her and rolls her eyes.	*The eye-rolling must be seen for exactly what it is: \an intentional act of overt incivility. It is in the same category as verbal threats and criticism. Most patterns of uncivil behavior are more subtle/passive and considered covert such as refusing to help, isolating or excluding the student, or ignoring your opinions.*
	In order to fully understand incivility, it must first be properly defined. Incivility "is defined as rude or disruptive behaviors that often result in psychological or physiological distress for the people involved and, if left unaddressed, may progress into threatening situations" (Clark, 2013).
	Bullying is similar to incivility and is defined in the literature as a consistent pattern of inappropriate abusive/aggressive behavior toward another colleague that is designed to:
	Intimidate
	Control
	Diminish
	Devalue
	Disrespect (Cooper & Curzio, 2012)
	Though a single episode of eye rolling is NOT a pattern, it clearly and intentionally communicates disrespect and is a rude behavior that will likely cause emotional stress to an inexperienced nursing student. Stydents typically are insecure because they know all too well what they don't know. They require care and SUPPORT from the clinical educator and the nurses they work with. When this is not present, the emotional consequences can be devastating.
She gives a quick report to Cindy, does not maintain eye contact, and promptly hurries down the hall stating she has to get to work or she will get behind.	*It is important to emphasize the flip-side to incivility which is CIVILITY! Civility can be defined by an attitude of RESPECT for one another, open/honest communication, working together, and respecting differences (Clark, 2013)*
	This response by the nurse confirms that the eye-rolling was likely no

	accident. *These behaviors communicate a devaluing and unwillingness to truly collaborate and work together in the care of the patient she has been assigned. As a result, the student likely feels isolated and unsupported. The student will likely feel hesitant to ask any questions because of what she has just experienced. Incivility in practice not only affects the nurses but also impacts patient safety and must not be tolerated.*

II. The Dilemma Begins…

Current Concern:

Cindy completes her initial assessment of her patient, a 68-year-old woman who presented to the hospital with a ruptured appendix and is now post-operative day one. Her temperature has increased to 101.2 (last recorded was 99.5), her heart rate is 98 (last recorded was 76) and her blood pressure is 98/60 (last recorded was 120/66). Cindy just had a classroom lecture on sepsis and the inflammatory response. Though an inflammatory response is expected after surgery, the instructor emphasized that systemic inflammatory response syndrome (SIRS) is an early predicator for sepsis that could progress to septic shock. SIRS criteria include temperature >100.4, heart rate >90 and decreasing blood pressure.

Cindy approaches Jennifer to share her concern that her patient may be developing sepsis. Jennifer appears irritated, and states in an angry tone, "I was just in her room an hour ago and she looked just fine. I think you are overreacting. I've been a nurse for twenty years. Do you think a student knows more than me? I don't think so! I will check on her when I get a chance."

What data from the current concern is important & RELEVANT; therefore it has clinical significance to the nurse?

RELEVANT Data from Current Concern:	Clinical Significance:
Cindy completes her initial assessment of her patient, a 68-year-old woman who presented to the hospital with a ruptured appendix and is now post-operative day one.	*It is ALWAYS relevant to note the age of the patient and determine if they are a higher risk for complications because of their age. Of the five rights of clinical reasoning, the "right" patient must always be considered as one who may be at higher risk for an adverse outcome because of age or other factors such as altered immune status or chronic illnesses (Levett–Jones et al., 2010).* *Though 68 is not excessively elderly, it must be noted that she had a ruptured appendix and this makes her a high risk for the development of sepsis.*
Her temperature has increased to 101.2 (last recorded was 99.5), her heart rate is 98 (last recorded was 76) and her blood pressure is 98/60 (last recorded was 120/66).	*This cluster of data is a clinical red flag for the nurse in practice. Each of these vital sign parameters are trending in the wrong direction and are reflecting a patient who may be sliding into sepsis. If this is not recognized by the nurse, this patient can easily go into septic shock and die as a result. One of the key components of the clinical reasoning is the importance of trending all relevant clinical data. The student has done this and has recognized a potential complication.*
Cindy just had a classroom lecture on sepsis and the inflammatory response. Though an inflammatory response is expected after surgery, the instructor emphasized that systemic inflammatory response syndrome (SIRS) is an early predicator for sepsis that could progress to septic shock. SIRS criteria include temperature >100.4, heart rate >90 and decreasing blood pressure.	*Cindy is an excellent student who has been able to translate classroom knowledge to the clinical bedside. This is a key objective for every nursing student. The most important content must be deeply understood so that students can make this translation to the bedside, where it matters most. This is why every nurse educator must make it a priority to filter and decrease the amount of content so that this deep learning can take place!*
Cindy approaches Jennifer to share her concern that her patient may be developing sepsis.	*Cindy is doing the right thing by going directly to the nurse who is responsible for this patient. She has shared her concern. It is now up to the nurse to take responsibility for this information.*

| Jennifer appears irritated, and states in an angry tone, "I was just in her room an hour ago and she looked just fine. I think you are overreacting. I've been a nurse for twenty years. Do you think a student knows more than me? I don't think so! I will check on her when I get a chance." | Instead of validating Cindy's, Jennifer continues to demonstrate unprofessional and uncivil behavior. It is obvious that the uncivil behavior demonstrated that devalues, diminishes, and disrespects is also evident in this interaction. She does not value the data that Cindy has presented that in reality is a red flag that must be followed up on. Instead, the primary nurse blows her off, minimizes her concern, and is not in a hurry to validate the potential for a need to rescue this patient who is likely having a change of status. |

III. Resolving the Dilemma

1. Identifying data that is RELEVANT, what is the essence of this current dilemma?

There are two concerns in this clinical dilemma.

- **Incivility**

  The behavior by the primary nurse is disrespectful and clearly uncivil. This is creating a tenuous working relationship for the student and the nurse that may impact patient safety. This behavior must never be accepted or minimized by the student or the clinical educator.

- **Primary nurse unwillingness to validate student concern**

  The uncivil behavior by the primary nurse impacts how she perceives the student's recognition of a patient who is in need of rescue from a change in status. Because the student was not valued,, this attitude has carried over into the care of the patient. The nurse is not willing to quickly act and validate the concerns of the student. This is in essence a patient safety concern that must be acted upon. How can the student nurse be an advocate for her patient when the primary nurse is unwilling to collaborate?

2. What additional information is needed by the student that would help clarify the current dilemma?

- **Incivility**

  Does this nurse have a pattern of being uncivil to other nurses on her unit, but more importantly, to other students? If other students have had a similar experience, this nurse should not have students at any time in the future. It is emotionally unsafe for them. On the other hand, if this nurse has been a role model and has had collaborative relationships working with other students, the reason for her behavior today needs to be brought to her attention. Though it may be surprising, some nurses are completely unaware that they are treating others in a disrespectful manner. This information should be brought by the clinical educator to the charge nurse.

- **Primary nurse unwillingness to validate student concern**

  The professional nurse is in essence a lifeguard and must recognize a change of status when it occurs. Since the clock is already ticking on a likely change of status, the student must ask how long it will be before the primary nurse is able to check on this patient. If the nurse is unwilling to clearly communicate this or continues to not value her insight, the student has the responsibility to go directly to her clinical instructor and work with her instructor to advocate for the patient. It would also be appropriate for the student to communicate any patient concerns FIRST to the clinical educator, who could corroborate the student's concern. Both of them would go directly to the primary nurse. This approach would likely be more effective in this situation.

3. What additional members of the healthcare team could be utilized in this situation? Why?

- **Nurse educator.**

  The clinical faculty is responsible for the students and the care that they provide. It would be totally appropriate for the student to come first to the clinical educator and work together on the clinical concern. Though there may be friction between the student and the staff nurses, students must know and understand that the clinical educator is an advocate for the student in this situation.

- **Charge nurse.**

  The charge nurse is the manager of the clinical shift. Any legitimate concerns that impact patient care are this person's concern. This is not triangulation, but following the chain of command when the primary nurse does not act in the best interests of the patient or has been disrespectful and uncivil to this student.

- *Nurse manager*

  Any significant concerns between a student and the unit staff ultimately need to be communicated to the nurse manager so they are kept in the loop. This is important especially if follow-up is needed for an incident that may develop from this scenario.

4. What is the priority?

- *Incivility*

  Student emotional safety.

  Students are especially vulnerable to experiencing incivility because some nurses perceive them as being a lower rank as a caregiver. The student must immediately communicate any perception or communication of disrespectful behavior by any nurse on the unit that impacts his/her ability to have a collaborative working relationship with the clinical faculty.

- *Primary nurse unwillingness to validate student concern*

  Failure to rescue.

  The patient's well-being and safety is at risk if a change of status is not immediately recognized and acted upon. Any delay by the primary nurse is not acceptable. The student must do everything possible to advocate for the patient by immediately communicating her concerns to her clinical educator.

5. What interventions and/or principles can be used by the student to successfully resolve this clinical dilemma?

- *Incivility*

  Because bullying thrives in an environment of passivity where it has become normalized, it often stops when it is addressed in an assertive, direct, and respectful way (Griffin, 2004). In one study where nurses were empowered by this strategy, 100 percent of the nurses reported that when the perpetrator was confronted, the bullying behavior stopped (Coursey, Rodriguez, Dieckmann, & Austin, 2013). This is an effective intervention that can be implemented if incivility is experienced. For example, if a bullying nurse has a pattern of raising eyebrows or other nonverbal innuendo toward you, be prepared to respond in the following manner, "I sense (I see from your facial expression) that there may be something you wanted to say to me. Please speak directly to me" (Coursey, Rodriguez, Dieckmann, & Austin, 2013).

  This approach is best implemented by staff nurses in practice to address incivility because there is a power imbalance. A student is at an immediate disadvantage because of this imbalance and her or his current role. It would be best in this situation for the student to promptly communicate any perception or uncivil behavior to the clinical faculty who can then address these concerns directly to the charge nurse or the primary nurse.

- *Primary nurse unwillingness to validate student concern*

  The student must immediately communicate this concern to the clinical educator. Once this has been done and the student and educator work together, they can approach the primary nurse and communicate any concerns. If the primary nurse continues to minimize the clinical situation, it would be appropriate for the clinical instructor to notify the charge nurse of the concern and let this person address it with the primary nurse so that any need for rescue can be quickly facilitated.

6. What is the expected response that would indicate interventions were effective?

- *Incivility*

  Incivility thrives when it is not directly addressed. If addressing the concern directly to Jennifer was effective, an attitude of collaboration and respect would be the fruit that this uncivil interaction which started off the day badly, would not have to continue to define that clinical day. It is important to assume the best in others and not the worst. Therefore, give the primary nurse a measure of grace and the opportunity to make needed amends with the student. Hopefully, all can put this in the rearview mirror!

- *Primary nurse unwillingness to validate student concern*

  If the primary nurse respectfully acknowledges the clinical concern and promptly assesses the patient, this would clearly indicate that this set of interventions were effective.

7. What is the student likely experiencing/feeling right now in this situation?

The consequences of incivility are devastating. They create feelings of inadequacy in a new nurse. Bullying is like putting gas on the fire of inadequacy. Feelings of failure, decreased self-esteem, self-doubt, anger, depression, burnout, and even post-traumatic stress disorder (PTSD) are common (Bartholomew, 2006). This leads to decreased morale, low job satisfaction, increased absenteeism, and ultimately leaving the unit or even nursing entirely (Murray, 2008). Thirty percent of new nurses leave their first job after the first year when bullying is personally experienced (Johnson & Rea, 2009).

Does this toxic environment impact patient care? Absolutely! The Joint Commission has taken the position that bullying is a safety issue and has issued a standard to that effect. It has been shown that a unit that has a prevalence of bullying behaviors can lead to increased medical errors, adverse patient outcomes, and lower rates of nurse retention. By creating an environment that does not make it safe to ask questions, incivility poses a serious threat to patient safety and overall quality of care (Johnson & Rhea, 2009).

Though workplace bullying occurs in all work settings, healthcare occupations have the highest rates of bullying (Johnson & Rhea, 2009). Surveys have shown that 93 percent of nurses have witnessed bullying and 85 percent reported that they were victims of bullying (Coursey, Rodriguez, Dieckman, & Austin, 2013). Sixty-four percent of nurses cited this as the primary reason for leaving their current job (Stagg, Sheridan, Jones, & Speroni, 2011). New nurses as well as men in nursing (Dellasega, 2009) are more likely to experience incivility most often from other more experienced or senior nurses (Griffin, 2004).

To put an exclamation point on how incivility emotionally impacts nurses, I want to share a letter written by a nurse colleague who was willing to share her experience as a new nurse right after graduation. Though her experience may seem extreme, it is tragically all too common. It is imperative for every educator and student to commit to being the change needed to stomp out this stain on our profession!

One New Nurse's Experience of Incivility:

I started on the unit with a fresh and positive attitude directly out of school. I thought I had found my dream job. However, I quickly learned that there was something incredibly dysfunctional about this unit. I had heard of 'horizontal violence' in nursing school, but I never expected that it would happen to me regularly in my own career and on my own unit. I have found this unit to be one of the most hostile, cold, unprofessional, passive-aggressive, inappropriate, and dysfunctional nursing units I have ever worked on. I find the unit to operate under a 'good old boys' mentality, where new staff fall victim to senior staff until they have 'proved themselves' or 'done their time' like they had to do.

I can honestly say that I cried every shift I worked for the first 6 months, and the only reason I stopped crying was not because it got any better, but because I had to change my expectations about the unit and accept my reality. I cannot put into words what it feels like to have nurses laugh in your face and belittle you when you ask a clinical question, roll their eyes and walk out on your report before it is finished, to literally have a back turned on you when trying to discuss a concern, or to be scolded or yelled at in front of your other colleagues until you are apologizing profusely with tears streaming down your cheeks.

There have been countless times that I have overheard slanderous things said about me or some of my other colleagues, and the unit has accepted this kind of behavior as acceptable. Individuals, including management, have chosen to turn a blind eye to the dysfunction on the unit, which then gives individuals the false impression that this kind of behavior is acceptable. In order to survive on the unit I have had to learn which of my colleagues I can utilize as resources and positive resources and those that I cannot have contact with under any circumstances because they are toxic to me and toxic to the unit.

I struggle to deal with the fact that a hospital with such a great reputation would allow such behaviors and dysfunction to go on. I have been actively applying for other positions for over a year, and if the economy was not the way it was, I and MANY of my colleagues would have left the unit. I think that speaks for itself. I have watched many situations in the past year and a half where individuals have gone to management, HR, or the union and they have been horribly retaliated against by 'the good old boys.' At this time I am not interested in making things any more difficult for myself. I would just like to get off of the unit before I lose my passion for nursing altogether.

8. What are the uncivil behaviors demonstrated by the staff nurse in this situation?
Incivility "is defined as rude or disruptive behaviors that often result in psychological or physiological distress for the people involved and, if left unaddressed, may progress into threatening situations" (Clark, 2013).
Bullying is similar to incivility and is defined in the literature as a consistent pattern of inappropriate abusive/aggressive behavior toward another colleague that is designed to:

Intimidate
Control
Diminish
Devalue
Disrespect (Cooper & Curzio, 2012)

The essence of the uncivil behavior in this situation can be summed up as DISRESPECT!

Though a single episode of eye rolling is NOT a pattern, it clearly and intentionally communicates disrespect. It is a rude behavior that will likely cause emotional stress to an inexperienced nursing student. Students are typically insecure because they know all too well what they don't know. Students require care and SUPPORT from both the clinical educator and the nurses they work with. When this is not present, the emotional consequences can be devastating.

Allow students to express their understanding and perspective of incivility or bullying. Build on this knowledge and understanding with a definition from the literature. Nurse educator and researcher Cynthia Clark has published and conducted the most research on this topic. Be aware of her work as well as her website, Civility Matters. It is an excellent resource site for both educators and students. Her book, "Creating and Sustaining Civility in Nursing Education" is a must-read for those who want to deepen their understanding of this relevant topic in nursing.
The address to her website Civility Matters is: **http://hs.boisestate.edu/civilitymatters/**

Other specific examples from the literature most commonly seen in the clinical setting include:
- Having information withheld so it affects your performance
- Having your views and opinions ignored
- Being personally ignored or excluded
- Micromanagment of your work
- Persistent criticism of your work and effort
- Having insulting/offensive remarks made about you
- Repeated reminders of your errors and mistakes
- Having false allegations or accusations made against you (Johnson & Rea, 2009)

9. Have you personally experienced uncivil or bullying behaviors? If so, how did it make you feel?
Because incivility is unfortunately endemic in much of the nursing profession, do not be surprised if many students who have worked as a nursing assistant or in other health-related context have experienced incivility and the emotional pain and consequences that it afflicts. Give your students a voice and have a rich discussion and dialogue over their experiences. Do not to dwell on them, but learn from them and help your students to resolve never to be that nurse regardless of the stress or difficulties they may experience in practice.

10. What was learned from this case study that you will incorporate into your practice?
Content knowledge without personal application will not be fruitful. Reflection is an essential professional behavior that can also be practiced! I have added this question to allow students to intentionally reflect on what they have learned so that they can integrate this essential content into their practice and fully develop the ethical comportment of the professional nurse. This question will facilitate rich dialogue in whatever context you choose to use this case study. If there is not enough time to discuss this question, consider having students write a one-page reflection paper.

References

Bartholomew, K., (2006), *Ending nurse to nurse hostility: Why nurses eat their young and each other.* Marblehead, MA: HCPro Incorporated.

Clark, C. (2013). *Creating and sustaining civility in nursing education,* Indianapolis, IN: Sigma Theta Tau International Publishing.

Cooper, B. & Curzio, J. (2012). Peer bullying in a pre-registration student nursing population, *Nurse Education Today, 32,* 939-944.

Coursey, J.H., Rodriguez, R.E., Dieckmann, L.S., & Austin, P.N. (2013). Successful implementation of policies addressing lateral violence, *AORN Journal, 97*(3), 101-109.

Dellasega, C.A. (2009). Bullying among nurses, *American Journal of Nursing, 109,* 52-58.

Griffin, M. (2004). Teaching cognitive rehearsal as a shield for lateral violence: An intervention for newly licensed nurses, *The Journal of Continuing Education in Nursing, 35,* 257-263.

Johnson, S.J. & Rea, R.E. (2009). Workplace bullying: Concerns for nurse leaders, *The Journal of Nursing Administration, 39*(2), 84-90.

Levett-Jones, T., Hoffman, K., Dempsey, J., Yeun-Sim Jeong, S., Noble, D., Norton, C. Hickey, N. (2010). The 'five rights' of clinical reasoning: An educational model to enhance nursing students' ability to identify and manage clinically 'at risk' patients. *Nurse Education Today, 30,* 515–520.

Murray, J.S. (2008). No more nurse abuse, *American Nurse Today,* 17-19.

Stagg, S.J., Sheridan, D., Jones, R., & Gabel Speroni, K. (2011). Evaluation of a workplace bullying cognitive rehearsal program in a hospital setting, *The Journal of Continuing Education, 12*(9), 395-401.

NURSE Dilemma

Student to Faculty Incivility

STUDENT Worksheet

Susan Sandstrom, 21 years old

Overview

Incivility continues to be a problem in nursing education. This dilemma identifies the most common uncivil behaviors that students demonstrate toward faculty and even other students. This activity will increase student awareness of incivility so unprofessional attitudes and behaviors are recognized, remedied and replaced with an attitude of respect.

Clinical Dilemma Activity: STUDENT
Student to Faculty Incivility
I. Scenario
History of Present Problem:
Susan Sandstrom is a 21-year-old first year nursing student at a local community college. She consistently received As without having to study at length in high school, and continues to work 20-30 hours a week as a nursing assistant to avoid having student loan debt. Nursing is a much more difficult major than she expected and she has been overwhelmed by the amount of content that she needs to know and the hours of studying required. Despite using all available time in her schedule to study, Susan has been averaging 80% on her exams. If she does poorly on the final, she may fail the program.

Susan has been increasingly frustrated by Joan, her current classroom instructor, whom she feels is the reason for her poor examination grades this semester. Instead of addressing her concerns directly to Joan, Susan openly shares her negative opinions of Joan to other students, as well as on her Facebook page. Numerous students share her negative assessment of Joan and "like" her comment that "Joan is the worst instructor ever who should go back to clinical practice where she belongs."

What data from the histories is important & RELEVANT; therefore it has clinical significance to the nurse?

RELEVANT Data from Present Problem:	Clinical Significance:

II. The Dilemma Begins...
Current Concern:
Though Joan is a clinical expert in ICU where she practiced for over twenty years, this is her second year teaching. Susan begins coming late to class, and texting on her cell phone to other students even when Joan is lecturing. Joan is reviewing the most recent exam questions with the class when Susan raises her hand and states, "That question was written so poorly. I can show you from the textbook that your answer is not the only correct one. If you've never taught this content before, how can you be so sure that you got this one right?"

What data from the current concern is important & RELEVANT; therefore it has clinical significance to the nurse?

RELEVANT Data from Current Concern:	Clinical Significance:

III. Resolving the Dilemma

1. Identifying data that is RELEVANT, what is the essence of this current dilemma?

2. What additional members of the nursing department could be utilized in this situation? Why?

3. What is the priority?

4. What interventions and/or principles can be used by both the student and educator to successfully resolve this dilemma?

5. What is the expected response that would indicate interventions were effective?

6. What is the faculty likely experiencing/feeling right now in this situation?

7. What is the student likely experiencing/feeling right now in this situation?

8. What are the uncivil behaviors demonstrated by the student in this situation?

9. How could civility be experienced in this situation instead of incivility?

10. What have you learned from this case study that you will incorporate into your practice?

NURSE Dilemma

Student to Faculty Incivility

Susan Sandstrom, 21 years old

Answer Key

Student to Faculty Incivility

I. Scenario

History of Present Problem:

Susan Sandstrom is a 21-year-old first year nursing student at a local community college. She consistently received As without having to study at length in high school, and continues to work 20-30 hours a week as a nursing assistant to avoid having student loan debt. Nursing is a much more difficult major than she expected and she has been overwhelmed by the amount of content that she needs to know and the hours of studying required. Despite using all available time in her schedule to study, Susan has been averaging 80% on her exams. If she does poorly on the final, she may fail the program.

Susan has been increasingly frustrated by Joan, her current classroom instructor, whom she feels is the reason for her poor examination grades this semester. Instead of addressing her concerns directly to Joan, Susan openly shares her negative opinions of Joan to other students, as well as on her Facebook page. Numerous students share her negative assessment of Joan and "like" her comment that "Joan is the worst instructor ever who should go back to clinical practice where she belongs."

What data from the histories is important & RELEVANT; therefore it has clinical significance to the nurse?

RELEVANT Data from Present Problem:	Clinical Significance:
Susan is a 21-year-old first year nursing student at a local community college.	*Just as the age of the patient is always relevant, the age of the student is also relevant. Because of lived life experiences, older students tend to be more resilient and mature in the academic process while younger students may struggle at times with a mature response to the stresses in academia.*
She consistently received As without having to study at length in high school, and continues to work 20-30 hours a week as a nursing assistant to avoid having student loan debt.	*In my own experience as an educator, I have observed that straight-A high school students will not always be straight-A students in nursing school. Many students find this major much more difficult than expected. For the first time, they have to study hard in order to maintain their grades.*
Nursing is a much more difficult major than she expected and she has been overwhelmed by the amount of content that she needs to know and the hours of studying required.	*Though some students must work to support a family or other financial needs, working 20 hours a week or less will ensure a higher likelihood of success in nursing education. Susan is likely working too many hours and should consider cutting to be successful. These boundaries are typically communicated in orientation, but many students think that they may be the exception and can even work full-time and still be able to develop their learning.*
Despite using all available time in her schedule to study, Susan has been averaging 80% on her exams. If she does poorly on the final, she may fail the program.	*This response is not uncommon for most nursing students. Nursing is typically the most difficult major in any college or university. Students can be overwhelmed and experience high levels of stress as a result. The amount of time that is required to study is also unexpected, and students struggle to find the time to meet in this ongoing demand.*
Susan has been increasingly frustrated by Joan, her current classroom instructor, whom she feels is the reason for her poor examination grades this semester.	*When a student who has been successful in the past is not able to maintain a grade that they feel they deserve or are capable of, they have two choices:* *First, take responsibility to master the content adequately to meet the objectives of the program. Reflect and determine if the study skills are effective or if they need to be modified. Effective studying skills are essential to student success. There are numerous resources at any college or university to assist students if they are struggling in this area.* *The second response is to blame the nursing program or nursing instructor they feel may be the reason for their lack of success.*

Instead of addressing her concerns directly to Joan, Susan openly shares her negative opinions of Joan to other students, as well as on her Facebook page.	*When a student chooses this response, it is too easy to fail to address this perception or her struggle privately with the faculty to work out any differences and empower Susan to make changes to be successful.*
	Professional communication is direct communication! *Unfortunately, some students find it much easier to be indirect and go to anyone except the person they have a perceived problem with. This behavior is not only unprofessional, but is uncivil and bullying. Gossip is commonplace in our culture, and social media facilitates this bad behavior. It is imperative that students hold themselves to the highest standards of professional behavior while in nursing school, so that they will be nurses of the highest professional standards after they graduate. If uncivil behavior is not corrected in nursing education, this student will continue to be part of the ongoing problem of incivility in nursing.*
	By sharing her negative opinions openly and freely with other students on social media using her Facebook page, Susan has crossed a line. Her behavior is representative of bullying behavior that can and will directly affect the reputation of this instructor. It is also a violation of the student policy handbook and will likely have consequences when this is discovered.
Numerous students share her negative assessment of Joan and "like" her comment that "Joan is the worst instructor ever who should go back to clinical practice where she belongs.	*Because Susan has chosen not to be direct with Joan about her concerns and her struggles as a nursing student, she finds artificial support among her friends who are all too willing to be sympathetic to her struggle. When other students choose to be sympathetic and "like" unprofessional behavior, it only encourages and perpetuates it.*
	The best professional and expected response whenever a student talks negatively about another student or nursing educator is to encourage that person to go directly to the source. If other students choose to listen and encourage and affirm Susan's concerns, they unknowingly become part of the problem and share in her incivility.

II. The Dilemma Begins…

Current Concern:

Though Joan is a clinical expert in ICU where she practiced for over twenty years, this is her second year teaching. Susan begins coming late to class, and texting on her cell phone to other students even when Joan is lecturing. Joan is reviewing the most recent exam questions with the class when Susan raises her hand and states, "That question was written so poorly. I can show you from the textbook that your answer is not the only correct one. If you've never taught this content before, how can you be so sure that you got this one right?"

What data from the current concern is important & RELEVANT; therefore it has clinical significance to the nurse?

RELEVANT Data from Current Concern:	Clinical Significance:
Though Joan is a clinical expert in ICU where she practiced for over twenty years, this is her second year teaching.	*Just as no one is born a nurse but requires education as well as experience to become proficient and master what is needed for practice, the same is true for nurse educators. No nurse educator is perfect. Most choose to become an educator because they have a passion and a love of learning and want to share their knowledge with the next generation. It is essential to assume the best of others not the worst. By assuming the worst of this educator, Susan has begun the downward spiral of incivility. Because they have a current or recent lens of clinical practice, they have a salience and relevance that students as well as educators*

	must recognize, acknowledge, and value.
Susan begins coming late to class, and texting on her cell phone to other students even though Joan is lecturing.	The anger and frustration that Susan continues to experience is reflected in these examples of the most common uncivil behavior that students demonstrate to faculty in nursing education. When viewed through the lens of RESPECT, it is apparent that each of these behaviors demonstrate an obvious disrespect for the instructor.
Joan is reviewing the most recent exam questions with the class when Susan raises her hand and states, "That question was written so poorly. I can show you from the textbook that your answer is not the only one correct. If you've never taught this content before how can you be so sure that you got this one right?"	Incivility tends to travel on a continuum of behaviors that begin with more passive and indirect patterns of incivility such as gossip. . But if left unattended, incivility can progress to more extreme and direct behaviors that include challenging the faculty member's knowledge or blatantly disrespectful attitudes and comments. Susan's response clearly demonstrates an adversarial and disrespectful attitude and is a RED FLAG. It is a more extreme form of incivility. This must be addressed directly and respectfully or it could progress even further to physical threats or violence.

III. Resolving the Dilemma

1. Identifying data that is RELEVANT, what is the essence of this current dilemma?
Student to faculty incivility that is progressing in severity that needs to be directly addressed.

2. What additional members of the nursing department could be used in this situation? Why?
Department chair or team leader (if present)
Once Susan's uncivil behavior of mobilizing student opinion against Joan as well as the inappropriate Facebook page is brought to the attention of the department, it will be clear that Susan's inappropriate and unprofessional use of social media has violated the department's code of ethics. In order to communicate the severity of this behavior, it is important to keep departmental leadership in the loop and to document this situation as it unfolds.

3. What is the priority?
Susan's uncivil behavior must be privately and directly addressed. A clear communication of acceptable boundaries and student accountabilities must be communicated to her. She must be held to the conduct outlined in the nursing student manual. Because of the more extreme level of incivility that was present in the classroom, it would be appropriate to include the team lead or the departmental chair when the student is brought in to address these concerns.

4. What interventions and/or principles can be used by both the student and educator to successfully resolve this dilemma?
- *Compare the difference between uncivil behavior and the desired outcome of civility.* Once a meeting can be arranged to directly address incivility, Susan's behavior can be compared and contrasted with the professional conduct that is expected of a student. The code of conduct outlined not only in the student handbook, but more importantly, the standards of the nursing profession have been violated. The American Nurses Association ANA code of conduct for the professional nurse also affirms the importance of caring and implied respect in all interactions with colleagues:
    - "The nurse maintains compassionate and caring relationships with colleagues and others with a commitment to the fair treatment of individuals, to integrity-preserving compromise, and to resolving conflict"
- *Choose respect.* Clark (2008) has identified that a dance of civility or incivility can take place in nursing education depending on the presence or absence of RESPECT. If educators treat students with respect, respect is much more likely to be given back in return. Conversely, if educators treat students with disrespect, disrespect and with it uncivil behaviors are much more likely and will continue to perpetuate. Doing all that is needed to encourage a culture of respect will have the power to change the culture of any nursing department.
- *Maintain and uphold the standards of behavior.* These standards are communicated in the student handbook with specific consequences for Susan's behavior. The entire program is watching. If a parent does not maintain

stated boundaries with an adolescent, they will soon be violated. The same is true in nursing education. As long as boundaries of behavior are followed through with the consequences that are outlined in the manual, whatever Susan experiences is deserved and will hopefully lead to a change of heart.

- ***Maintain an attitude of grace.*** *Just as Jesus challenged the crowd that wanted to stone the woman caught in the act of adultery by asking, "He who is without sin, cast the first stone" (John 8:7), I believe that it is imperative to give Susan this same measure of grace and understanding. But don't forget that Jesus also said to the same woman after all her accusers all departed, "Go and sin no more!" (John 8:11) In the same way, Susan must also recognize the consequences of her behavior and must resolve to make needed changes.*
- ***Teach students strategies to manage stress.*** *Since nursing education is a high stakes major with high levels of stress experienced by both faculty and students, practical tools and strategies to manage stress should be addressed on the first day in orientation!*

Remember that unless another student makes faculty aware of the earlier uncivil behavior demonstrated by Susan, the faculty who are affected by these uncivil behaviors are not even aware of the problem so it can be addressed! This is an excellent reason why it is imperative for other students to hold their peers to the highest level of professional behavior.

If negative gossip is heard about a student or faculty, this behavior can be directly and respectfully addressed by simply stating to the person slandering another, "It sounds like you have a situation that should be addressed specifically to that person. I don't see how your actions are going to resolve your concern. Why don't you take it to them directly and resolve this without including others in this discussion?" Standing up for the absent colleague is essential not only in nursing education, but also in clinical practice where uncivil behavior is common among nurses. Resolve to be a part of the needed change in nursing education while you are still a student so that you will have a positive impact as a nurse in practice!

5. What is the expected response that would indicate interventions were effective?
An interesting observation about uncivil behaviors is that when a person who is perpetrating and responsible for this behavior is directly confronted, the uncivil and bullying behavior will stop in most instances. When this behavior goes on unchallenged and becomes part of a cultural norm, it flourishes. IIf Susan's bullying and uncivil behavior ceases, but more importantly, demonstrates a change of heart by Susan asking forgiveness and apologizing for her conduct, this is a reflection of the deeper heart change that one would desire in this situation.

6. What is this faculty likely experiencing/feeling right now in this situation?
A recent study confirmed that the effects of uncivil behavior from students have numerous emotional and even physical consequences. Faculty expressed being anxious, worried, intimidated, stressed, upset, and dread coming to work. Some even had physical effects such as migraines, inability to sleep, and episodes of crying. Some faculty question their desire to continue to teach after experiencing uncivil students and leave academia altogether.

7. What is the student likely experiencing/feeling right now in this situation?
Though Susan is experiencing high levels of stress and feeling overwhelmed byin the program, this is never an excuse for uncivil behavior. What is not known is her response to being directly confronted with uncivil behavior. Is she remorseful? Would she do things differently? Use this as a discussion question to see the range of emotion that students in your class or clinical setting would have if they were responsible for this type of behavior and were required to explain or justify what they did and why.

8. What are the uncivil behaviors demonstrated by the student in this situation?
Allow students to express their understanding and perspective of incivility or bullying. Build on this knowledge and understanding that a student may have with a definition from the literature. Nurse educator and researcher Cynthia Clark has published and conducted the most research on this topic. Be aware of her work as well as her website, Civility Matters, is an excellent resource site for both educators and students. Her book, "Creating and Sustaining Civility in Nursing Education," is a must-read for those who want to deepen their understanding of this relevant topic in nursing. The address to her website Civility Matters is: ***http://hs.boisestate.edu/civilitymatters/***

Incivility "is defined as rude or disruptive behaviors that often result in psychological or physiological distress for the people involved and, if left unaddressed, may progress into threatening situations" (Clark, 2013).

Bullying is similar to incivility and is defined in the literature as a consistent pattern of inappropriate abusive/aggressive behavior toward another colleague that is designed to:

Intimidate

Control

Diminish

Devalue

Disrespect (Cooper & Curzio, 2012)

The following are the most common examples of student to faculty incivility in the literature (those in this case study are in bold)

- *Disruptive behaviors in class/clinical that include*
  - *Rude comments, engaging in side conversations, dominating class*
  - ***Cell phone, texting***, *inappropriate computer use in class*
  - ***Late to class*** *and leaving early*
  - *Sleeping in class (Clark & Springer, 2010)*
- *Anger or excuses for poor performance*
- *Inadequate preparation (Clark, 2008)*
- *Pressuring faculty until they get what they want (Clark, 2008)*
- ***Bad-mouthing other students, faculty, and the nursing program*** *(Clark, 2008)*

9. How could civility be experienced in this situation instead of incivility?

CIVILITY is RESPECT for others while honoring differences and seeking common ground with colleagues. It requires tolerating, listening, and being able to discuss differing viewpoints respectfully and treating one another with dignity and honor. (Clark & Carnosso, 2008).

Civility must always be the end objective for the culture that is desired in nursing education by both students and faculty. To create a culture of civility, any department can implement the following are practical steps n:

- ***Create a culture of caring and respect.*** *Respect and value the differences of others and their uniqueness as a human being. Thank God that we are not all the same and celebrate this diversity! This is a good thing but also a source of friction especially when the stakes are high as well as the levels of stress!*

- ***Model what you want your students to become.*** *Faculty must embrace their responsibility to lead by example and demonstrate respect and caring behaviors with all interactions between students and colleagues.*

- ***Support your students as well as each other.*** *When incivility is experienced by faculty, the educator will need support and affirmation of his or her value and importance to the department. Even Solomon recognized the wisdom of this when he wrote, "Two are better than one ‥ for if they fall, one will lift up his fellow. But woe to him who is alone when he falls and has not another to lift him up!" Ecclesiastes 4: 9-10*

Words that are spoken are a two-edged sword. They can bring healing or they can deeply wound. In childhood, there was a common saying, "Sticks and stones may break my bones but words can never hurt me!" Unfortunately, this statement is a lie, because words do hurt, and disrespectful words or words spoken in anger have a power to become our identity and the way we view ourselves. Because so much hinges on our words and how we communicate with one another, we must strive to be QUICK to listen and SLOW to speak!

Solomon, the wisest man of ancient history, wrote the following words of wisdom. If put into practice, they will also work to recapture civility in nursing and nursing education. I have found the following principles of communication life-giving and restorative if they are used consistently in all that we say and do with our students and to one another.

Our words have power

"There is that speaketh like the piercings of a sword: but the tongue of the wise is health." Proverbs 12:18

Our tone matters

"A soft answer turneth away wrath: but grievous words stir up anger." Proverbs 15:1

- *Be proactive, Discuss best practice in the literature regarding the most effective ways to handle student incivility when it occurs so that faculty are empowered and can more effectively manage it if it presents again in the future.*

10. What have you learned from this case study that you will incorporate into your practice?
Content knowledge without personal application will not be fruitful. Reflection is an essential professional behavior that can also be practiced! I have added this question to allow students to intentionally reflect on what they have learned so that they can integrate this essential content into their practice and fully develop the ethical comportment of the professional nurse. This question will facilitate rich dialogue in whatever context you choose to use this case study. If there is not enough time to discuss this question, consider having students write a one-page reflection paper.

References

Clark, C. M. (2008). The dance of incivility in nursing education as described by nursing faculty and students. *Advances in Nursing Science*, 31, E37–E54.

Clark, C. (2013). Creating and sustaining civility in nursing education, Indianapolis, IN: Sigma Theta Tau International Publishing.

Clark, C. M. & Springer, P.J. (2010). Academic nurse leaders' role in fostering a culture of civility in nursing education, *Journal of Nursing Education,* 49(6), 319–325.

Clark, C. M. & Carnosso, J. (2008). Civility: A concept analysis. Journal of Theory Construction & Testing, 12, 11–15.

Cooper, B. & Curzio, J. (2012). Peer bullying in a pre-registration student nursing population. *Nursing Education Today,* 32(8), 939-944.

NURSE Dilemma

Faculty to Student Incivility

STUDENT Worksheet

John Hedstrom, 35 years old

Overview

Though incivility is endemic in nursing practice, it is also evident in nursing education and directed from students to faculty, faculty to students, and faculty to faculty. This case study identifies the most common uncivil behaviors that students may experience from nursing faculty and shows them how to resolve this situation directly and respectfully so that a culture of civility can be realized in nursing education.

Faculty to Student Incivility

I. Scenario

History of Present Problem:

John Hedstrom is a 35-year-old second year student at a local community college. He is going back to school after working as a paramedic the past 12 years. He is an engaged student who is excited to build on his knowledge and experience as a paramedic to become a flight nurse or nurse anesthetist. He is not afraid to ask questions in theory to clarify his understanding of content. His current classroom instructor, Helen, has been a nurse educator for thirty years. She answers the questions of other students in class, but when John asks more than one question in lecture, she becomes obviously irritated. When she is unable to answer his question, she tells him to go find it on the Internet and look it up himself.

In today's lecture on shock, Helen has a slide that states that the heart rate decreases in progressive and irreversible shock. When John raises his hand to clarify this information that contradicts what he has seen in practice as a paramedic, Helen replies harshly, "You are a student in nursing school! Just because you have been a paramedic does not mean that you know it all!" Since this last interaction, John has not asked another question in class.

What data from the histories is important & RELEVANT; therefore it has clinical significance to the nurse?

RELEVANT Data from Present Problem:	Clinical Significance:

II. The Dilemma Begins…

Current Concern:

Helen is John's clinical instructor. He has noticed that she does not spend as much as time to develop his learning compared to the other students who are women in his clinical group. When John has his mid-clinical evaluation with Helen, she tells him, "Men go into nursing only for the money. You don't show that you care, and all you really seem to focus on is understanding the pathophysiology of each patient you care for. I don't think you have what it takes to be a good nurse."

What data from the current concern is important & RELEVANT; therefore it has clinical significance to the nurse?

RELEVANT Data from Current Concern:	Clinical Significance:

III. Resolving the Dilemma

1. *Identifying data that is RELEVANT, what is the essence of this current dilemma?*

2. *What additional members of the nursing department could be used in this situation? Why?*

3. *What is the priority?*

4. *What interventions and/or principles can be utilized by both the student and educator to successfully resolve this dilemma?*

5. *What is the expected response that would indicate interventions were effective?*

6. *What is the faculty likely experiencing/feeling right now in this situation?*

7. *What is the student likely experiencing/feeling right now in this situation?*

8. *What are the uncivil behaviors demonstrated by faculty in this situation?*

9. *How could civility be experienced in this situation instead of incivility?*

John Hedstrom, 35 years old

Answer Key

Clinical Dilemma Activity: ANSWER KEY

Faculty to Student Incivility

I. Scenario

History of Present Problem:

John Hedstrom is a 35-year-old second year student at a local community college. He is going back to school after working as a paramedic the past 12 years. He is an engaged student who is excited to build on his knowledge and experience as a paramedic to become a flight nurse or nurse anesthetist. He is not afraid to ask questions in theory to clarify his understanding of content. His current classroom instructor, Helen, has been a nurse educator for thirty years. She answers the questions of other students in class, but when John asks more than one question in lecture, she becomes obviously irritated. When she is unable to answer his question, she tells him to go find it on the Internet and look it up himself.

In today's lecture on shock, Helen has a slide that states that the heart rate decreases in progressive and irreversible shock. When John raises his hand to clarify this information that contradicts what he has seen in practice as a paramedic, Helen replies harshly, "You are a student in nursing school! Just because you have been a paramedic does not mean that you know it all!" Since this last interaction, John has not asked another question in class.

What data from the histories is important & RELEVANT; therefore it has clinical significance to the nurse?

RELEVANT Data from Present Problem:	Clinical Significance:
John is a 35-year-old second year student at a local community college. He is going back to school after working as a paramedic the past 12 years.	*John is an older second career student who has valuable life experience as a paramedic. Though the scope of practice is dramatically different, his paramedic experience and his encounters with life-threatening patient care scenarios will benefit and deepen his learning as a nursing student.*
He is an engaged student who is excited to build on his knowledge and experience as a paramedic to become a flight nurse or nurse anesthetist. He is not afraid to ask questions in theory to clarify his understanding of content.	*John is engaged in his learning and as a result asks numerous questions to deepen and clarify his knowledge. It is not uncommon for men to be more assertive and willing to ask questions in the classroom.*
His current classroom instructor Helen, o has been a nurse educator for thirty years. She answers the questions of other students in class, but when John asks more than one question in lecture, she becomes obviously irritated. When she is unable to answer his question, she tells him to go find it on the Internet and look it up himself.	*Her response to John is a potential red flag for faculty incivility. Faculty incivility can include showing favoritism or being reluctant or unwilling to answer questions (Clark, 2008). Her nonverbal behavior and irritation is also a concern. Though the answer to his question may be appropriate, the tone appears unnecessarily harsh.*
In today's lecture on shock, Helen has a slide that states that the heart rate decreases in progressive and irreversible shock. When John raises his hand to clarify this information that contradicts what he has seen in practice as a paramedic, Helen replies harshly, "You are a student in nursing school! Just because you have been a paramedic does not mean that you know it all!"	*The content on this slide is clearly inaccurate. John is not being a smart-Alec, but appears to be matter-of-factly clarifying what is an obvious contradiction to what he has seen in practice. Even the classic pathophysiologic formula of $CO=SV \times HR$ has relevance to this slide because, as shock progresses, the expected physiologic response is to elevate heart rate in order to maintain cardiac output. Student put-downs or devaluing prior John's prior life experiences as a paramedic are additional examples of faculty incivility in the literature (Clark, 2011).*
Since this last interaction, John has not asked another question in class.	*This is tragic and can be attributed to the uncivil behavior of Helen. She has sent a message that his clarification and input in her class is not*

welcome. John has received this message loud and clear. Because men remain a gender minority in nursing as well as nursing education, it is not uncommon for the masculine distinctive that includes being assertive to be placed on the back burner. The message that men get from this type of faculty response is that they are expected to behave more like women, keep their heads low, and not make any waves to simply get through the program.

It is important to note that male nursing students are HIGH risk because they have some of the highest failure to complete nursing education rates of any demographic in nursing education today. In one study, the failure to complete rate for men was almost 30 percent; in comparison, women had a 10 percent failure to complete rate. The statistical relationship of gender and course completion in this same study was $p=0.009$ (McLaughlin, Muldoon, & Moutray, 2010)! These findings have been replicated. Male failure—to-complete rates remain as high as 40–50 percent in some programs.

II. The Dilemma Begins…

Current Concern:

Helen is John's clinical instructor. He has noticed that she does not spend as much as time to develop his learning compared to the other students who are women in his clinical group. When John has his mid-clinical evaluation with Helen, she tells him, "Men go into nursing only for the money. You don't show that you care, and all you really seem to focus on is understanding the pathophysiology of each patient you care for. I don't think you have what it takes to be a good nurse."

What data from the current concern is important & RELEVANT; therefore it has clinical significance to the nurse?

RELEVANT Data from Current Concern:	Clinical Significance:
Helen is John's clinical instructor. He has noticed that she does not spend as much as time to develop his learning compared to the other students who are women in his clinical group.	*This is a student observation that he does not get as much time with his instructor as female students. Based on his prior experience and Helen's uncivil behavior in the past, this assessment is likely accurate. Another aspect of faculty incivility is showing favoritism to other students. Though it is unclear if the uncivil behaviors that Helen has shown toward John are rooted in gender bias, this behavior remains disrespectful and uncivil.*
When John has his mid-clinical evaluation with Helen, she tells him, "Men go into nursing only for the money. You don't show that you care, and all you really seem to focus on is understanding the pathophysiology of each patient you care for. I don't think you have what it takes to be a good nurse."	*Helen's unfiltered comments make it very clear that her uncivil behavior is a reflection of bias against men in nursing. Unfortunately, this experience is not uncommon and remains a well-documented concern in the literature.*
	The literature supports that men do care, but they demonstrate this differently than women. Helen appears to have this unwarranted assumption that John does not care because he does not do it in a manner that is more representative of a feminine construct. For example, it has been shown that women are much more likely to use physical touch while caring for patients. Men are much less likely to use physical touch, but will use humor in order to establish a trust relationship with their patient.. It is important to recognize and respect the gender distinctives of both men and women in nursing education.
	In one qualitative study of male nursing students, Patterson et al., 1996, identified masculine caring by establishing a rapport with patients that was akin to friendship that was not dependent on the use of touch. In

	another study, men consistently used humor in their interactions with patients to develop a caring rapport. Thompson (2002) has observed that men tend to provide care from an emotionally safe distance. Men also are more likely to adopt a "professional model" of caregiving that equates nursing care as work and emphasizes task-completion and problem-solving to meet patient needs.
	Helen has also made another unwarranted assumption that it is a negative to focus on the pathophysiology of patients. Men tend to focus on the hard applied sciences of nursing versus the softer aspects of the profession. This is another masculine distinctive that needs to be understood and appreciated.
	Having a deep understanding of pathophysiology has direct relevance to John's nursing practice because it is this knowledge that will provide the critical thinking that will facilitate early recognition of a change of status and rescue a patient who develops a complication.
	Though faculty may have an opinion about the abilities of students, to tell John that he will not be a good nurse is another example of a put-down that is representative of faculty incivility.

III. Resolving the Dilemma

1. Identifying data that is RELEVANT, what is the essence of this current dilemma?
Faculty to student incivility that appears to be motivated by gender bias.

2. What additional members of the nursing department could be used in this situation? Why?
- ***Nursing department chair.*** *Instead of going directly to the Dean of the program, it is important for John to follow the chain of command. The uncivil and biased behavior that John has experienced is unacceptable and needs to be addressed to Helen. Because there is a power imbalance in nursing education between students and educators, based on his history with Helen, directly addressing his concerns with her will likely provoke further hostility and will not resolve this situation.*

3. What is the priority?
To communicate his lived experience of faculty incivility and likely gender bias to the department chair so that this uncivil behavior can be addressed and it ceases immediately.

4. What interventions and/or principles can be utilized by both the student and educator to successfully resolve this dilemma?
- ***Choose respect.*** *Clark (2008) has identified that a dance of civility or incivility can take place in nursing education depending on the presence or absence of RESPECT. If educators treat students with respect, respect is much more likely to be given back in return. Conversely, if educators treat students with disrespect, disrespect and with it uncivil behaviors are much more likely and will continue to perpetuate. Doing all that is needed to encourage a culture of respect will have the power to change the culture of any nursing department.*

  It is important for both parties, but especially Helen, to have an attitude of respect for all students and to treat them equally regardless of any personality conflict or gender.

5. What is the expected response that would indicate interventions were effective?
The uncivil and inappropriate behavior by Helen would cease immediately after any meeting between the student and nursing leadership took place. But more importantly, Helen needs to develop insight and understanding into her behavior, recognize that it is wrong, and ask for forgiveness from John. The goal is to build a bridge between faculty and students and a win-win.

6. What is the student likely experiencing/feeling right now in this situation?
Incivility typically creates feelings of inadequacy as well as feelings of failure, decreased self-esteem, self-doubt, anger, depression, burnout, and even post-traumatic stress disorder (PTSD.(Bartholomew, 2006) Ultimately, many leave nursing entirely (Murray, 2008). One of the feelings that men commonly experience is ambivalence about their decision to be a nurse. When difficulties such as faculty bias become apparent, instead of fighting, they choose to drop out quietly.

7. What are the uncivil behaviors demonstrated by faculty in this situation?
Use this opportunity to provide a summary of the bullet points that represent faculty to student incivility. This will also empower students to recognize if these characteristics and behaviors have been demonstrated by other faculty. Or, if these behaviors are experienced in the future, the student is empowered to directly and respectfully address this concern with nursing department leadership. In order to make civility a realistic attainment, the cancer of uncivil behavior must be identified and removed.

The following are the most common examples of faculty to student incivility in the literature (those in this case study are in bold)
- *Faculty superiority that is demonstrated by*
  - *Exerting position and control over students (Clark, 2008)*
  - *Setting unrealistic student expectations (Clark, 2008)*
  - *Assuming a "know-it-all" attitude (Clark, 2008)*
  - ***Being rigid, unapproachable, or rejecting students' opinions** (Clark, 2011)*
- ***Devaluing students' prior life experiences that can include work and academic experiences** (Clark, 2008)*
- *Ineffective educators who cannot manage the classroom (Clark, 2008)*
- ***Making condescending remarks or put-downs to students** (Clark, 2011)*
- ***Showing favoritism to certain students** (Clark, 2008)*
- ***Refusing or reluctant to answer questions** (Clark, 2011)*

8. How could civility be experienced in this situation instead of incivility?
CIVILITY is RESPECT for others while honoring differences and seeking common ground with colleagues. It requires tolerating, listening, and being able to discuss differing viewpoints respectfully and treating one another with dignity and honor. (Clark & Carnosso, 2008).

Civility must always be the end objective for the nursing culture. To create a culture of civility, any department can implement these practical steps to bring about a needed change in nursing education:
    ***Create a culture of caring and respect.** Respect and value the differences of others and their uniqueness as a human being. Thank God that we are not all the same and celebrate this diversity! This is a good thing but also a source of friction, especially when the stakes are high and raise stress levels!*
- ***Model what you want your students to become.** Faculty must embrace their responsibility to lead by example and demonstrate respect and caring behaviors with all interactions between students and colleagues.*

- ***Support your students as well as each other.** When incivility is experienced, students will need support and affirmation. Even Solomon recognized the wisdom of this when he wrote, "Two are better than one ¨for if they fall, one will lift up his fellow. But woe to him who is alone when he falls and has not another to lift him up!" Ecclesiastes 4: 9-10*

Words that are spoken are a two-edged sword. They can bring healing or they can deeply wound. In childhood, there was a common saying, "Sticks and stones may break my bones but words can never hurt me!" Unfortunately, this statement is a lie, because words do hurt, and disrespectful words or words spoken in anger have a power to become our identity and the way we view ourselves. Because so much hinges on our words and how we communicate with one another, we must strive to be QUICK to listen and SLOW to speak!

Solomon, the wisest man of ancient history, wrote the following words of wisdom in Proverbs that, if put into practice, will also work to recapture civility in nursing and nursing education. I have found the following principles of communication life-giving and restorative if they are used consistently in all that we say and do with our students and one another.

Our words have power
"There is that speaketh like the piercings of a sword: but the tongue of the wise is health." Proverbs 12:18

Our tone matters
"A soft answer turneth away wrath: but grievous words stir up anger." Proverbs 15:1

References

Bartholomew, K., (2006), *Ending nurse to nurse hostility: Why nurses eat their young and each other.* Marblehead, MA: HCPro Incorporated.

Clark, C. M. (2008). The dance of incivility in nursing education as described by nursing faculty and students. *Advances in Nursing Science, 31*, E37–E54.

Clark, C. M. (2011). Pursuing a culture of civility: An intervention study of one program of nursing, *Nurse Educator, 36*(3), 98–102.

Clark, C. M. & Carnosso, J. (2008). Civility: A concept analysis. *Journal of Theory Construction & Testing, 12*, 11–15.

McLaughlin, K., Muldoon, O.T., & Moutray, M. (2010). Gender, gender roles and completion of nursing education: A longitudinal study. *Nurse Education Today, 30,* 303–307.

Murray, J. S. (2008). No more nurse abuse. *American Nurse Today,* 17–19.

Paterson, B. L., Tschikota, S., Crawford, M., Saydak, M., Venkatesh, P., & Aronowitz, T. (1996). Learning to care: Gender issues for male nursing students. *Canadian Journal of Nursing Research, 28*(1), 25–39.

Thompson, E. H. (2002). What's unique about men's caregiving? In B. J. Kramer & E. H. Thompson (Eds.), *Men as caregivers: Theory, research, and service implications* (pp. 20–50). New York: Springer.

NURSE Dilemma

Student Burnout

STUDENT Worksheet

Susan Peterson, 21 years old

Overview

Most nursing students experience high levels of stress. For some, it crosses a line and the slow fade of burnout can steal the joy and passion of caring for others. Nursing has one of the highest rates of burn out of any profession. Identifying EARLY signs of burnout and practical strategies to cultivate self-care is required and is the emphasis of this nursing dilemma.

Student Burnout

I. Scenario

History of Present Problem:
Susan Peterson is a 21-year-old second year nursing student at a local community college who consistently received As in high school, but has been able to maintain only a C average since she began the program. She continues to work thirty hours a week as a nursing assistant to support herself. She wants to be the best nurse possible and if she does not raise her grades, her expectations and perceptions of herself are directly impacted. Though she has made adjustments in her study habits and feels she knows the content, her grades have not improved.

This additional stress has caused her to feel mentally and physically exhausted even though she feels that she is getting enough sleep. She has neglected to take time to attend church or maintain relationships outside of school this past semester because "I don't have the time."

What data from the histories is important & RELEVANT; therefore it has clinical significance to the nurse?

RELEVANT Data from Present Problem:	Clinical Significance:

II. The Dilemma Begins...

Current Concern:
Susan comes to clinical and appears physically tired. Michelle, the clinical instructor becomes concerned when she observes Susan respond harshly to her patient's request for a pain medication. After clinical, Michelle asks Susan if everything is alright. Susan begins to break down and cry and tells Michelle, "I feel like such a failure! What was I thinking even going into this program. I feel so helpless. Regardless of all that I do, I can't even get a B in my major!"

What data from the current concern is important & RELEVANT; therefore it has clinical significance to the nurse?

RELEVANT Data from Current Concern:	Clinical Significance:

III. Resolving the Dilemma

1. Identifying data that is RELEVANT, what is the essence of this current dilemma?

2. What additional information is needed by the nurse that would help clarify the current dilemma?

3. What additional members of the educational team could be used in this situation? Why?

4. What is the student priority?

5. What interventions and/or principles can be utilized by the student to successfully resolve this clinical dilemma?

6. What is the expected response of the student that would indicate the interventions were effective?

7. What response by the student would indicate that additional interventions are needed?

8. What is the student likely experiencing/feeling right now in this situation?

9. What are some practical self-care strategies you could implement to minimize or put out the potential fire of burnout while a student?

NURSE Dilemma

Student Burnout

Susan Peterson, 21 years old

Answer Key

Clinical Dilemma Activity: ANSWER KEY

Student Burnout

I. Scenario

History of Present Problem:

Susan Peterson is a 21-year-old second year nursing student at a local community college who consistently received As in high school, but has been able to maintain only a C average since she began the program. She continues to work thirty hours a week as a nursing assistant to support herself. She wants to be the best nurse possible and if she does not raise her grades, her expectations and perceptions of herself are directly impacted. Though she has made adjustments in her study habits and feels she knows the content, her grades have not improved.

This additional stress has caused her to feel mentally and physically exhausted even though she feels that she is getting enough sleep. She has neglected to take time to attend church or maintain relationships outside of school this past semester because "I don't have the time."

What data from the current concern is important & RELEVANT; therefore it has clinical significance to the nurse?

RELEVANT Data from Current Concern:	Clinical Significance:
Susan is a 21-year-old second year nursing student at a local community college who consistently received As in high school, but has been able to maintain a C average since she began the program.	*For most students this is a source of ongoing stress and anxiety. Especially if the C average is close to the failing percentage.*
She continues to work thirty hours a week as a nursing assistant to support herself.	*There are only 24 hours in each day and 168 hours in a week. Working 30 hours a week with school, studying, sleep and needed blank or quiet space or margin will make it a challenge for Susan to spin all of these platters successfully. Though some students do not have an option to decrease their work schedule due to family and income obligations, if at all possible, fewer than 20 hours a week of outside work is the recommended maximum so that student learning and its resultant impact on patient care is not affected. Nursing education must be a priority, but balanced with other life priorities for each student as well.*
She wants to be the best nurse possible and if she does not raise her grades, her expectations and perceptions of herself are directly impacted.	*There is a red flag in this statement. Though many students want a good grade, there are some that wrap their value and self-worth as a student and even as a person in the grade they receive. Some students have excessively high expectations of themselves, and when these expectations are not met, it can create a devastating blow to their self-image and self-worth as a person.*
Though she has made adjustments in her study habits and feels she knows the content, her grades have not improved.	*Though she is making needed change in her study habits as well as her knowledge of the content, it has not impacted her grades which are extremely important to her. This will be an ongoing source of anxiety and additional stress.*
This additional stress has caused her to feel mentally and physically exhausted even though she feels that she is getting enough sleep.	*This is another red flag. There is a temptation to make a trade-off when there is not enough time in the day to accomplish what the student may feel is most important.*
She has neglected to take time to attend church or maintain relationships outside of school this past semester because "I don't have the time."	*There was an article written years ago called the Tyranny of the Urgent http://static1.squarespace.com/static/52f11228e4b0a96c7b51a92d/t/5321d9a8 e4b053c8acec66b0/1394727336868/Tyranny+of+the+Urgent.pdf that beautifully captures this dilemma. There will always be urgent matters*

	that demand one's attention. But if we allow the urgent to dictate our responses to life, the most important things can be easily neglected because they do not require an immediate urgency. This is especially true with maintaining one's spiritual life and practices. Because they are not urgent, they can easily be neglected.

II. The Dilemma Begins…

Current Concern:

Susan comes to clinical and appears physically tired. Michelle, the clinical instructor becomes concerned when she observes Susan respond harshly to her patient's request for a pain medication. After clinical, Michelle asks Susan if everything is alright. Susan begins to break down and cry and tells Michelle, "I feel like such a failure! What was I thinking even going into this program. I feel so helpless. Regardless of all that I do, I can't even get a B in my major!"

What data from the current concern is important & RELEVANT; therefore it has clinical significance to the nurse?

RELEVANT Data from Current Concern:	Clinical Significance:
Susan comes to clinical and appears physically tired.	*It is not uncommon for students to be physically tired especially if they have an early morning clinical. But in this situation, this could be an early presentation of burnout. There are five stages to burnout that typically follow one another. The first stage is mental and physical exhaustion. Ironically, most nursing students are already in that first stage and need to be on guard against the progression and slow fade that burnout represents.* *Nurses have one of the highest rates of burnout among all healthcare professionals. This can be attributed in part to the tendency for many nurses to put the needs of others ahead of their own. Added to this is the ongoing emotional strain of caring for patients who are sick, dying, or demanding (Alexander, 2012).* *Burnout has been described as the progressive loss of the initial idealism, passion, energy, and purpose to enter the profession (Edelwich, 1980). It can also be defined as the loss of human caring, or stated another way, the separation of caregiving and caring (Benner & Wrubel, 1989).* *Burnout has five distinct stages that represent a predictable progression. Teach your students the key characteristics that each stage represents to identify burnout EARLY and prevent needless progression.* ***Stage 1*** • *Mental and physical exhaustion* • *Emotional emptiness* • *Little or no desire to relate or engage with patients* ***Stage 2*** • *Indifference* • *Cynical, uncaring* • *Dehumanize patient and family* ***Stage 3*** • *Feelings of failure as a nurse* • *Feelings of helplessness* ***Stage 4*** • *Feelings of failure as a person* • *Self-hatred, isolation* • *Increased absenteeism from work*

© 2015 Keith Rischer/www.KeithRN.com

157

	Stage 5 (complete burnout)
	• *Performs responsibilities of nurse with no involvement, commitment, or enthusiasm*
	• *Completely disengaged*
	• *Contemplates leaving nursing (Spinetta et al., 2000)*
Michelle, the clinical instructor, becomes concerned when she observes Susan respond harshly to her patient's request for a pain medication.	*Though Susan's response to her patient may be a result of her physical tiredness, it is a clinical red flag that must not be ignored. Uncaring behaviors present in the second stage of burnout. When this data is clustered with her current stress levels related to her grades and physical exhaustion, Susan is a candidate for progressive burnout.*
After clinical, Michelle asks Susan if everything is alright. Susan begins to break down and cry and tells Michelle, "I feel like such a failure! What was I thinking even going into this program. I feel so helpless. Regardless of all that I do, I can't even get a B in my major!"	*This response clearly confirms the educator's suspicion that Susan is in crisis as a result of the stressors as a student and the progression of burnout. The third stage of burnout includes feelings of failure as a nurse as well as helplessness. These feelings are clearly expressed by Susan and confirm her current struggle. Left unattended the fire of burnout will eventually consume and impact the entire structure of a person's being.*

III. Resolving the Dilemma

1. Identifying data that is RELEVANT, what is the essence of this current dilemma?
Susan is currently experiencing progressive burnout as a result of not only the stress of the nursing program, but her unrealistic expectations and the need to have better grades in order to validate her sense of value and worth as a nurse and a human being.

Susan is working 20+ hours a week. For some students, working this much may lead to overload and trigger burnout given who they are and the limits of what is humanly possible for them to accomplish.

2. What additional information is needed by the nurse that would help clarify the current dilemma?
Allow Susan to communicate her feelings and whatever she is comfortable sharing. It is important to take time to have a conversation and for faculty to hear from the student's perspective what is going on in their lives.

3. What additional members of the educational team could be used in this situation? Why?
- ***Team lead or department chair.*** *Meeting privately with the student is the first step. Then one can involve the department leadership so they are aware of this student crisis and can document it. If faculty spread the burden, it benefits the student. For example, two people might meet with the student at one time. (Two faculty or faculty and team lead/director). This may help the student develop an awareness of the seriousness of the situation and prompt the student to act responsibly to make changes in their life related to educational success. It is the student who has the problem and ultimately needs to fix the problem, but faculty must make the student aware and offer resources for successful outcomes. Debriefing the student can assist in coping with stressful situations (Yoder, 2010).*

- ***Student services.*** *It may go by different names depending on the college or university, but the organization that could provide referrals or provide resources should be involved. Student services have a wealth of resources that many times go untapped because faculty doesn't refer students in a timely manner or student struggles go unidentified. Better to refer one too many than one too few students for assistance. (Counseling, financial assistance, referrals, etc.) Once students arrive at the door of student services, they return with a plan, peace of mind and changed perspective.*

- ***Local pastor.*** *Coping strategies noted by Yoder include prayer, faith, and time with a pastor (2010). Nursing students can pray for themselves and others. Knowing that Susan has a church affiliation, an emotional crisis often impacts and has spiritual implications that could be alleviated by pastoral counsel and guidance.*

Frequently, these situations are complex until the correct identification of the problem/problems is made by the student/faculty unit, it is challenging to move forward. This may take some outside intervention and collaboration, but ultimately the responsibility for the outcome lies with the student and the choices they make. Students may struggle with owning their behavior and choices. It may be their poor choices that got them into the dilemma and it takes new behaviors to work out of the situation. Learning new behaviors takes time and practice and doesn't happen with stating the obvious only one time. That is where team, collaboration, and self-reflection are required and necessary in a nurse's skill set. We need to be there to help them in this developmental process.

4. What is the student priority?
Caring and support from the nursing department as well as guidance from a professional counselor may be needed to examine priorities. If a student knows that they are supported by the nursing department, this will be a strength that she can lean on to get through this.

"I don't have the time" is a red flag that Susan's time management skills need to be examined. What are her priorities and what simple changes can she make to de-stress her life? Students struggle with owning the choices they make related to priorities in their lives. The first step might for Susan be to see that something must go to make room for nursing school and its rigors. Twenty hours of work a week may be more than she can handle.

5. What interventions and/or principles can be used by the student and/or faculty to successfully resolve this clinical dilemma?
Student
- **Seek help**... *have a plan and a timeline for the plan*
- **Own the problem.** *Faculty do not own this problem and are not responsible for the outcome. The student owns the problem and faculty have a responsibility to track the student and offer resources to help the student succeed.*

Faculty
- *Demonstrate caring behaviors that clearly communicate that Susan is being supported*
- *Provide Susan with the name, phone numbers, or website addresses of organizations that can support her in the community and the possible need for counseling*

6. What is the expected response of the student that would indicate the interventions were effective?
Burnout has predictable stages. It is apparent that Susan is in stage III and approaching stage IV because of her feelings of failure as a person as well as a nurse. If the fire is put out because the supportive and caring interventions were effective, feelings of failure would diminish in their intensity and she would be able to see herself as a person of value and worth regardless of her grade.
Additional expected responses include:
- *Susan succeeds in making lifestyle changes and successfully passes the course. Remind students that no one asks what grade you received in a certain course or exam once one leaves nursing school.*
- *Susan begins to have realistic expectations of herself.*

7. What response by the student would indicate that additional interventions are needed?
If Susan continues to maintain feelings of helplessness and failure as a person or nurse, this would be a clinical red flag. Additional signs of stage IV burnout include self-hatred, isolation, or disengagement from the academic setting.

8. What is the student likely experiencing/feeling right now in this situation?
Susan is obviously overwhelmed, exhausted emotionally, physically, and even spiritually. Her self-worth and value as a person is tied disproportionately to her grade, not for the value that she currently has as a human being created in the image of God.

9. What are some practical self-care strategies you could implement to minimize or put out the potential fire of student burnout?
The topic of self-care and practical strategies to effectively manage stress is a MUST to address on the first day of orientation for every new student. To maintain a healthy balance to prevent burnout in practice, students must recognize the value of self-care and it needs to begin while they are in nursing school! This is a struggle for most students and

nurses. Though this new career path will consume them with new challenges and additional learning, some students need permission to NOT let nursing education become their life! Students need to take time to smell the roses along the way in life and balance this with academic rigor. Many nurses struggle with this at times. It is best to learn this life lesson earlier rather than later.

Encourage your students to pursue and fight for the balance that is needed by establishing "margins" in their life. Margin is the space between our current demands and our limit to handle them (Swenson, 2004). Those blank spaces on the sides of each page have a purpose as do margins or blank spaces in our daily life. If we continually push ourselves to the point of our load limit, we will soon find out that this cannot be sustained for any length of time. This, too, is a life skill that must FIRST be modeled and lived out by faculty!

The perpetual "gerbil wheel" that students are on in academia with its incessant, ongoing demands requires students to be fully aware of the need to renew their body, mind, and spirit. If they have not made this a priority, encourage them to recognize the connection between caregiving and giving of themselves as they care (Tanner, 2004). Just as educators give of themselves as they teach, nurses in practice do the same. If the "tank" of personal renewal is empty or dangerously low, this will directly impact the ability to be fully engaged and caring in practice.

The following are specific strategies that should be communicated to students (and lived out by faculty!) to empower them to make changes and adjustments as they enter the profession. More importantly, these same strategies can also be applied in the midst of academia, which is inherently stressful for students as well as nurse educators.

Personal Lifestyle Strategies
- **Obtain adequate sleep.** The magic number is SEVEN hours of sleep minimum every night. Remind your students that adequate amount of sleep is the easiest way to prevent emotional and physical exhaustion.
- **Eat healthy.** The common saying, "Garbage in, garbage out" certainly has relevance here! Encourage your students to see it as well!
- **Engage in regular physical activity.** Thirty minutes of sustained activity three to five times a week is needed for health and stress reduction. For those who are exercise-averse, a brisk walk is just as effective! Have your students look up the pathophysiology of endorphins and the secondary benefits this provides as well!
- **Identify what is MOST important in life and make time for it.** I readily identify with students who are highly driven and task/goal-oriented and who struggle to achieve balance. Though successfully completing nursing education is important, spouses, children, and friendships require QUANTITY time, not just quality to thrive..
- **Nurture your spirituality.** In addition to cultivating your spiritual life for balance and purpose in life, the importance of spirituality has relevance to patient care as a nurse. In order to provide meaningful spiritual care in the clinical setting, this priority needs to be "in you" (Remember the old Michael Jordan and Gatorade commercials?)
- **Participate in outside interests.** It's tempting for some students to keep the pedal to the metal and make nursing school their life. Although we want our students to be committed and serious about their education, we must also emphasize the importance of BALANCE.
- **Recognize limitations.** Some students will push themselves to the brink of exhaustion to pursue perfection as a student. As a nurse educator, do not assess solely a student's aptitude and ability as a nurse, but step back and assess their emotional health and how they handle the stresses of nursing education. Have this on your radar and do not hesitate to "go there" and discuss these principles of self-care in your classroom or clinical situations, or individually as needed (Alexander, 2012).

Professional/Educational Lifestyle Strategies
- **Set realistic goals of your current abilities.** This is especially important to discuss with your high-achieving students who have consistently attained a high GPA in high school or other programs and now find themselves with a GPA that is lower than they may have ever had. Encourage them to recognize the difficulty of the nursing major, and readjust their GPA goal to reflect their current reality.
- **Seek support of colleagues or other students.** The relevance of this principle was also validated over 2,500 years ago from Ecclesiastes in the Old Testament: "Two are better than one... For if they fall, the one will lift up his fellow: but woe to him that is alone when he falleth; for he hath not another to help him up" (Ecclesiastes 4:9–10).

- *Grieve well.* Nurses should never remain oblivious or indifferent to the pain and suffering of others whom they encounter in practice. Encourage students to remain empathetic, but also provide practical guidance and needed support when grief or painful feelings need to be addressed.
- *Take breaks as needed.* Students need to make time for rest, hobbies, relationships, faith, and any other interests that are important to them. Many students are highly driven, and need to be reminded that what comes naturally may not benefit them in practice. I have found the book <u>Margin: Restoring Emotional, Physical, Financial, and Time Reserves to Overloaded Lives</u> helpful in this ongoing battle for balance

---

References

Alexander, L. L. (2012). Burnout–impact on nursing. Retrieved from http://www.netce.com/coursecontent.php?courseid=827

Benner, P. & Wrubel, J. (1989). *Primacy of caring: Stress and coping in health and illness.* Menlo Park, CA: Addison-Wesley Publishing Company.

Edelwich J. & Brodsky, A. (1980). *Burn-out: Stages of Disillusionment in the Helping Professions.* New York, NY: Springer.

Spinetta, J. J., Jankovic, M., Ben Arush, M. W., et al. (2000). Guidelines for the recognition, prevention, and remediation of burnout in health care professionals participating in the care of children with cancer: report of the SIOP Working Committee on Psychosocial Issues in Pediatric Oncology. *Medical and Pediatric Oncology, 35*(2), 122–125.

Swenson, R. (2004). *Margin: Restoring emotional, physical, financial, and time reserves to overloaded lives.* Colorado Springs, CO: NavPress.

Tanner, C. A. (2004). The meaning of curriculum: Content to be covered or stories to be heard? *Journal of Nursing Education, 43*(1), 3–4.

Yoder, E.A. (2010). Compassion fatigue in nurses, *Applied Nursing Research,* 23, 191-197.

Recommended Resources for Nurse Educators

As a newer nurse educator who remains current in clinical practice, I have found the following resources helpful, relevant and NEED to read! They will empower any nurse educator to acquire a deeper understanding of what is required to more effectively teach as well as transform nursing education.

Nursing Education

- Attewell, A. (2012). *Illuminating Florence: Finding Nightingale's legacy in your practice.* Indianapolis, IN: Sigma Theta Tau International.
- Benner, P. (1982). From novice to expert. *American Journal of Nursing, 82*(3), 402–407.
- Benner, P., Sutphen, M., Leonard, V., & Day, L. (2010). *Educating nurses: A call for radical transformation.* San Francisco, CA: Jossey-Bass.
- Benner, P., Hooper-Kyriakidis, P., & Stannard, D. (2011). *Clinical wisdom and interventions in acute and critical care: A thinking-in-action approach.* (2nd ed.). New York, NY: Springer.
- Bussard, M.E. (2015). Clinical judgment in reflective journals pf prelicensure nursing students. *Journal of Nursing Education.54,* 36-40.
- Clarke, S.P. & Aiken, L.H. (2003). Failure to rescue. *American Journal of Nursing, 103,* 42-47.
- del Bueno, D. (2005). A crisis in critical thinking. *Nursing Education Perspectives, 26*(5), 278–282.
- Koharchik, L., Caputi, L., Robb, M., & Culleiton, A.L. (2015). Fostering clinical reasoning in nursing students. *American Journal of Nursing, 115,* 58-61.
- Levett-Jones, T., Hoffman, K., Dempsey, J., Yeun-Sim Jeong, S., Noble, D., Norton, C. Hickey, N. (2010). The 'five rights' of clinical reasoning: An educational model to enhance nursing students' ability to identify and manage clinically 'at risk' patients. *Nurse Education Today, 30,* 515–520.
- Scanlon, J. M., Care, W. D., & Gessler, S. (2001). Dealing with the unsafe student in clinical practice, *Nurse Educator, 26*(1), 23–27.
- Swanson, K. M. (1991). Empirical development of a middle range theory of caring. *Nursing Research, 40*(3), 161–166.
- Swanson, K. M. (1999). *What is known about caring in nursing: A literary meta-analysis.* In A.S. Hinshaw, S.L. Feetham, & J.L.F. Shaver, eds. *Handbook of clinical nursing research.* Thousand Oaks, CA: Sage Publications.
- Tanner, C. A. (1990). Caring as a value in nursing education. *Nursing Outlook, 38*(2), 70–72.
- Tanner, C. A. (2006). Thinking like a nurse: A research-based model of clinical judgment in nursing. *Journal of Nursing Education, 45*(6), 204–211.

Civility

- Clark, C. M. (2008). The dance of incivility in nursing education as described by nursing faculty and students. *Advances in Nursing Science, 31,* E37–E54.
- Clark, C. (2013). *Creating and sustaining civility in nursing education,* Indianapolis, IN: Sigma Theta Tau International Publishing.
- Clark, C. M. (2013). National study on faculty-to-faculty incivility: Strategies to foster collegiality and civility. *Nurse Educator, 38*(3), 98–102.

- Clark, C. M., Olender, L., Kenski, D., & Cardoni, C. (2013). Exploring and addressing faculty-to-faculty incivility: A national perspective and literature review. *Journal of Nursing Education, 52*(4), 211–218.
- Goldberg, E., Beitz, J., Wieland, D., & Levine, C. (2013). Social bullying in nursing academia. *Nurse Educator, 38*(5), 191–197.
- Griffin, M. (2004). Teaching cognitive rehearsal as a shield for lateral violence: An intervention for newly licensed nurses. *The Journal of Continuing Education in Nursing, 35*, 257–263.
- Heinrich, K. T. (2006). *Joy-stealing games.* Retrieved from the Reflections on Nursing Leadership Web site: http://www.reflectionsonnursingleadership.org/pages/vol32_2_heinrich.aspx

Men in Nursing

- Anthony, A.S. (2004). Gender bias and discrimination in nursing education: Can we change it?, *Nurse Educator, 29*, 121-125.
- Harding, T., North, N., & Perkins, R. (2008). Sexualizing men's touch: Male nurses and the use of intimate touch in clinical practice, *Research and Theory for Nursing Practice: An International Journal, 22*(2), 88-101.
- O'Lynn, C.E. (2004). Gender based barriers for male students in nursing education programs: Prevalence and perceived importance, *Journal of Nursing Education, 43*(5), 229-236.
- O'Lynn, C. (2012). *A man's guide to a nursing career.* New York, NY: Springer Publishing Company
- Roth, J.E., & Coleman, C.L. (2008). Perceived and real barriers for men entering nursing: Implications for gender diversity, *Journal of Cultural Diversity, 15*(3), 148-152.

Self-Care

- Hummel, C. (1967). Tyranny of the urgent. Retrieved from http://www.my279days.com/wp-content/uploads/2010/08/Tyranny-of-the-Urgent.pdf
- Swenson, R. (2004). *Margin: Restoring emotional, physical, financial, and time reserves to overloaded lives.* Colorado Springs, CO: NavPress.

Websites

- American Assembly for Men in Nursing: http://aamn.org/
- Civility Matters: http://hs.boisestate.edu/civilitymatters/
- Educating Nurses: http://www.educatingnurses.com/

My new book for students available only on KeithRN.com:

THINK
Like a Nurse!

Practical Preparation for Professional Practice

"As an experienced bedside nurse and educator, I have always tried to help the brand new nurse understand how to prioritize what actions are most critical. THINK like a Nurse! puts all of those concepts into clear, logical, and useable steps. My students really appreciate the clinical "pearls," the lab overviews, and the cardiac medication reviews. I will be using this book for all my new grads transitioning into practice."

-Willi Ellison, MSN, RN, CEN, CCRN, Residency Coordinator
Dignity Health/St. Rose Hospitals, Las Vegas, Nevada

"When I read THINK like a Nurse! my first thought was, "Wow! Where was this book when I was in nursing school?" I enjoyed how much of a condensed version of nursing school this book was. I would definitely recommend this book to my friends who are still in nursing school because I feel it would help benefit them and better prepare them for the "real" nursing world."

-Samantha Fernando, RN, New graduate residency program
St. Rose Dominican Hospital, Las Vegas, Nevada

This resource has been adopted as a required supplemental text by nursing programs across the country. Contact me (Keith@KeithRN.com) for special pricing for either eBook or textbook bundles!

Content Themes:

- Why caring & compassion is foundational not only to patient care, but how it benefits the nurse as well!
- Why the applied sciences of A&P, F&E, and pharmacology are essential to critical thinking and must be mastered by the new nurse. I identify the MOST important content of the sciences that must be mastered and why.
- Break down the complexity of how a nurse thinks at the bedside to recognize current care priorities through an emphasis of CLINICAL REASONING.
- Incivility and bullying is endemic in both nursing education and in practice. I discuss practical strategies to directly and respectfully address so that students are empowered as well as the historical legacy of men in nursing and breaking down current barriers that persist in nursing education.

Clinical Reasoning Case Study Workbooks

Available on KeithRN.com (store on homepage)

FUNDAMENTAL Reasoning (263 p.)

FUNDAMENTAL Reasoning is a basic, introduction to clinical reasoning that is best suited for the fundamental level. It emphasizes application of the applied sciences of pharmacology, dosage calculation, and F&E. Recognizing clinical relationships and identifying the nursing priority to establish a plan of care contextualized to the bedside.

RAPID Reasoning (281 p.) RAPID Reasoning is a "just right" length for most students, best suited for basic med/surg content. Each RAPID Reasoning case study situates essential content to the bedside, and incorporates the template of clinical reasoning questions that allows thinking to be practiced in the safety of the classroom.

UNFOLDING Reasoning (377 p.) UNFOLDING Reasoning is an advanced/synthesis level case study that contextualizes essential content to the bedside, and incorporates the template of clinical reasoning questions. In addition, a clinical change of status must be recognized as the scenario unfolds over time.

Clinical Reasoning Case Study Workbooks

Though there is an almost limitless number of topics that could be covered in nursing education, there are fewer concepts that must be mastered to prepare students for professional practice. I have created a workbook with twelve case studies that situate the most important concepts to practice. If your program utilizes a concept-based curriculum, these twelve examples will provide the contextualization hook that students require to acquire deep learning of what is most important. In addition to the paper workbooks, the electronic PDF files of the blank student version, faculty key, and concept/content map are included.

Each workbook has the same clinical scenario, but differing levels of complexity in the body of the clinical reasoning case study. This allows educators to level the content and complexity of nurse thinking throughout the program. I also have additional clinical reasoning case studies that can be purchased separately on the home page of KeithRN.

The following case study topics are included in this workbook series:

Unit 1: Fundamentals

- Surgical Pain Management (1 of 2)

Unit 2: Cardiovascular System

- Hypertension
- Acute Coronary Syndrome/Myocardial Infarction
- Heart Failure/Acute Renal Failure

Unit 3: Respiratory System

- Pneumonia/Chronic Obstructive Pulmonary Disease

Unit 4: Neurologic System

- Cerebral Vascular Accident

Unit 5: Digestive System

- Cirrhosis
- Pediatric Gastroenteritis

Unit 6: Endocrine System

- Diabetic Ketoacidosis/Chronic Renal Failure

Unit 7: Reproductive System

- Breast Cancer

Unit 8: Synthesis Clinical Reasoning Case Studies

- Sepsis/Septic Shock
- Narcotic Over Sedation/Cardiac Arrest (2 of 2)